AMAZING ALASKA!

FALL IN LOVE WITH ALASKA THROUGH
INTERESTING FUN FACTS AND FANTASTIC
STORIES FOR THE ENTIRE FAMILY

THE AMAZING STATES OF AMERICA SERIES

MARIANNE JENNINGS

KNOWLEDGE
NUGGET BOOKS

Copyright and Disclaimer

Amazing Alaska!
Fall in Love with Alaska through Interesting Fun Facts and Fantastic Stories for the Entire Family

Amazing States of America Series

Cover design by Paul Hawkins
Edited by Doreen Martens
Fact-checked by Hank Musolf

Library of Congress Control Number: 2023910590
ISBN 978-1-7342456-8-4 (paperback)
ISBN 978-1-7342456-9-1 (ebook)

Disclaimer:
Reader discretion is advised.

ALSO BY MARIANNE JENNINGS

So You Think You Know Canada, Eh?

Gold Medal Winner and **#1 Bestseller** in both Canadian Travel & Trivia and Fun Facts – This collection of silly & interesting facts is about Canada, the kind people who live there, all things maple syrup, hockey & lacrosse, its unique history, the breathtaking nature, & words to help you speak Canadian.

Available as a paperback and ebook.

Everything About Astronauts Vol. 1 & Vol. 2

Teens and adults who love astronauts, fun facts, and little-known stories will find themselves mesmerized with over 1,400 interesting facts and out-of-world stories.

Available as a paperback and ebook.

To Nome, my soulmate and perfect adventure buddy.

HOW TO READ THIS BOOK

This book is divided by topics, with links to jump to wherever you'd like.

There is no need to read this book cover to cover.

Just pick a subject that seems interesting and dig right in.

To test yourself and your friends with what you've learned, you'll find a fun, short quiz with answers in the back.

Bookmark All the Helpful Alaska Resources

Find all of the fun and helpful Alaska resources mentioned throughout this book (plus a few extras) including color images, videos, recipes, recommended Alaska Books and more at:

KnowledgeNuggetBooks.com/resources

TABLE OF CONTENTS

FREE SPECIAL BONUS

As a special bonus and as a **thank you for purchasing this book**, I created a FREE companion quiz e-book with over 100 fun questions and answers taken from this book.

Test your knowledge of Alaska and quiz your friends.

It's all FREE.

Download your bonus quiz e-book here:

http://bit.ly/alaskabook-bonus

Enjoy!

INTRODUCTION

So, you want to learn about the coolest state in the USA
(literally)! Alaska is not just a place. It's a whole different world
filled with bizarre and interesting facts that will blow your
mind.

Did you know that there are more caribou than people in
Alaska? Or that there's a tiny Alaskan town called Chicken,
where every summer the town organizes a musical festival
called Chickenstock? And how about the fact that Alaska has
the highest concentration of glaciers in the world? Yep, this
state is truly one-of-a-kind!

In this book, we'll take you on a wild ride through the wacky
world of Alaska, where the sun stays up all night in the
summer, and the northern lights dance in the winter. You'll
learn about the giant vegetables grown in the Matanuska Valley
(a 138-pound cabbage, anyone?), and the time when a town
elected a cat as their mayor.

We'll also delve into the fascinating cultures that call Alaska home, from the Yupik people of the Arctic to the Tlingit tribe of the Southeast.

So, whether you're a seasoned Alaskan adventurer or just curious about this fascinating state, get ready to be entertained and amazed by the quirkiest facts and stories that Alaska has to offer!

Enjoy!

ALASKA BASIC FACTS

ALASKA'S NAME AND WHAT IT MEANS

The word Alaska comes from the Aleut/Unangax̂ word alaxsxaq, meaning "the mainland." The literal translation is "the object towards which the action of the sea is directed." Alaska is also known as Alyeska, an Aleut word that means the "great land."

Aleut and Unangax̂ are names for the Indigenous people of the Aleutian Islands, located between the North Pacific Ocean and the Bering Sea.

ALASKA'S NICKNAME

Alaska is called "The Last Frontier" thanks to its thousands of square miles of rugged and magnificent wilderness, much of it uninhabited and largely unreachable by humans.

· · ·

ALASKA'S ORIGINAL INHABITANTS

A long time ago, over 15,000 years ago, the first people arrived in Alaska. They came from Siberia, crossing what's now known as the Bering Land Bridge, that connected it to Alaska. This land bridge is now underwater.

These first Alaskans were composed of various tribes and linguistic groups, such as the Inupiat, Yupik, Tlingit, Haida, Tsimshian, Athabaskan, and Aleut peoples. Each group developed unique cultural practices, social structures, and ways of living in harmony with the harsh Alaskan environment.

OUTSIDERS REACHED ALASKA IN 1741

Vitus Bering was a Danish explorer in the Russian navy who proved that a relatively narrow strip of sea divided the farthest reaches of Asia and North America. He led an expedition with Russian explorer Aleksei Chirikov in 1741 to explore what was east of Russia. During a storm, the two ships were separated. Chirikov sailed on to find some of the Aleutian Islands, while Bering recorded some of the western Aleutian Islands and Mount Saint Elias. Illness and harsh conditions brought an untimely end to the expedition, and Bering and 28 others died on an uninhabited island. The surviving men returned and reported the presence of potentially lucrative fur-bearing animals in the region.

Aleksei Chirikov was the first Russian to set eyes on the northwest coast of North America. After their ships were separated, Chirikov never saw Bering again.

DID YOU KNOW?

The Bering Strait, the Bering Sea, Bering Island, the Bering Glacier and Vitus Lake were all named after Vitus Jonassen Bering. The Bering Glacier and Vitus Lake are both in today's state of Alaska.

Chirikof Island, located in the Gulf of Alaska, and Mount Chirikov, a mountain in the Aleutian Range in Lake Clark National Park, were named after Aleksei Chirikov.

RUSSIAN FUR TRADERS HEAD TO ALASKA

For Russians, the main economic activity in the region was the fur trade, with sea otters being particularly profitable. Russian fur traders explored and established settlements in Alaska after Bering and Chirikov stumbled onto the region in 1741. The first permanent settlement was founded in 1784 at Three Saints Bay on Kodiak Island by Grigory Shelikhov.

RUSSIAN ORTHODOX MISSIONARIES AND DISEASE

Russians gradually expanded their presence in Alaska, created more settlements, and claimed more territory. They sent missionaries to convert Alaska Natives to Christianity and establish missions. However, Alaska's Native population was decimated by diseases such as smallpox and influenza that were

introduced by the Russians, for which they had no natural
immunity.

WANNA BUY ALASKA?

Russia had money problems in the mid-1800s, and the fur
trade in Alaska wasn't doing well. The Russian government
didn't think Alaska would be particularly profitable in the
future. It also worried about being unable to protect Alaska if
Britain (which claimed everything north of the 49th Parallel)
invaded. So in 1867, Russia asked the United States if it
wanted to buy Alaska for $7.2 million, and the answer was yes.

THE ALASKA PURCHASE

On March 30, 1867, Russia sold Alaska to the US for $7.2
million. This is about 2 cents per acre. In 2023 money, this is
equivalent to $144 million or 33 cents per acre.

JUST WRITE US A CHECK

The US purchase was transacted in the form of a check written
to Edouard de Stoeckl, the Russian diplomat who had
promoted and negotiated the deal on Russia's behalf. Today,
you can find the check in the National Archives in Washington
D.C., along with the Declaration of Independence, the Consti-
tution and the Bill of Rights.

*Cancelled check in the amount of $7.2 million, for the
purchase of Alaska, issued August 1, 1868. Source:
archives.org*

NOT A POPULAR PURCHASE

Not everyone was excited about the decision by the US Secretary of State, William Seward, to purchase Alaska. At the time, the deal was dubbed "Seward's Folly," "Seward's Icebox," and "Andrew Johnson's Polar Bear Garden" (Andrew Johnson being US president at the time).

When gold was discovered in 1880, those who had criticized the purchase decided it might have been a smart investment after all.

THE MANY NAMES OF ALASKA

After the purchase from Russia, it became known as the Department of Alaska, from 1867 until 1884. In 1884, administration of the area was reorganized and it was given a new name, the District of Alaska. In 1912, Alaska was again renamed the Territory of Alaska. It wasn't until 1959 that Alaska finally became a state.

· · ·

ALASKA IS THE 49TH STATE

Alaska officially became a state on January 3, 1959, and with that increased the size of the United States by nearly one-fifth.

ALASKA'S HARD-TO-REACH STATE CAPITOL

Juneau, located in the southeast region of Alaska, is the only US capital not accessible by car. Juneau can only be reached by hopping on a plane or taking a boat.

HOW ALASKA IS DIVIDED UP

To wrap your head around the massive state that is Alaska, it helps to know that Alaska has six regions:

- Southeast Alaska
- Southcentral Alaska
- The Interior
- Alaska's Arctic
- Southwest Alaska
- Western Alaska

ALASKA DOESN'T HAVE COUNTIES; IT HAS BOROUGHS

Rather than being divided by county, like every other American state except Louisiana (which has parishes), Alaska has 19 boroughs and one "Unorganized Borough."

. . .

Boroughs don't cover the entire land area of the state. The more densely populated regions are included in the 19 boroughs, which have organized area-wide governments and operate similarly to counties in other states. The rest of the state belongs to the Unorganized Borough.

Within the Unorganized Borough, there is no local government, but services are provided by the state of Alaska.

TIME ZONES

Alaska used to have four time zones, but that was condensed to two in 1983. Most Alaskans, including those in Anchorage, Juneau and Fairbanks, follow Alaska Standard Time, which is one hour behind the West Coast of the US, or nine hours behind Coordinated Universal Time (UTC-9).

The western part of the state, including the Aleutian Islands, is in the Hawaii-Aleutian Time Zone, which is two hours behind the West Coast, or 10 hours behind Coordinated Universal Time (UTC-10).

DAYLIGHT SAVINGS TIME

Alaska participates in Daylight Saving Time, like the majority of the US states, from March to November.

THE LANGUAGES OF ALASKA

Alaska has at least twenty-one official languages. In 1998, English was designated the official state language. But in 2014, a bill added 20 Alaska Native tongues as co-official state languages. In 2021, 15.7 percent of Alaskans identified as American Indian or Alaska Native, the highest of any state.

ALASKA STATE SYMBOLS

Alaska's state symbols are the Sitka spruce (state tree), dog mushing (state sport), the moose (state land animal), bowhead whale (state marine animal), jade (state gem), gold (state mineral), the forget-me-not (state flower), king salmon (state fish), Alaskan malamute (state dog) and the willow ptarmigan (state bird).

THE FLAG OF ALASKA WAS DESIGNED BY A 14-YEAR-OLD

In 1927, the Seward Gateway newspaper announced a competition to design a flag for Alaska, which was still a US territory at the time. The contest was opened to all 7th- to 12th-grade (12- to 18-year-old) students in the territory.

Roughly 700 designs were submitted, with 142 submissions being sent for final selection. Of those 142, the winning design featured eight stars to represent the Big Dipper, placed on a blue background to represent the sky and the forget-me-not flower. The winner was 14-year-old Benny Benson, a boy of mixed Unangax̂, Swedish and Russian heritage who had grown up in an orphanage after his mother died.

*Benny Benson holding his winning Alaska State Flag
design. Source: Alaska State Library.*

Along with an illustration of his design, Benny wrote this
explanation:

---

*"The blue field is for the Alaska sky and the forget-me-
not, an Alaska flower. The North Star is for the future of
the state of Alaska, the most northerly in the Union. The
dipper is for the Great Bear—symbolizing strength."*

For his winning flag design, Benson won a $1,000 scholarship
and a watch with the flag emblem on it. He used the scholar-
ship to study diesel mechanics. His design was adopted as the
official state flag in May 1927 and flown for the first time the
following July 9. It's still used today.

· · ·

ALASKA'S MOTTO

Alaska's State Motto is "North to the Future," which reflects the idea of Alaska as a land of promise and opportunity. As with the flag, the motto was chosen in a 1967 contest sponsored by the Alaska Centennial Commission to celebrate 100 years since the Alaska purchase. Richard Peter, a Juneau-based journalist, was the winner.

ALASKA'S STATE SONG

Alaska's state song is "Alaska's Flag," composed by Elinor Dusenbury, whose husband was commander of Chilkoot Barracks at Haines from 1933 to 1936. The lyrics were written by Marie Drake, an Alaska Department of Education employee. It was adopted as the official state song in 1955.

> *Eight stars of gold on a field of blue,*
> *Alaska's flag, may it mean to you*
> *The blue of the sea, the evening sky,*
> *The mountain lakes and the flowers nearby,*
> *The gold of the early sourdough's dreams,*
> *The precious gold of the hills and streams,*
> *The brilliant stars in the northern sky,*
> *The "Bear," the "Dipper," and shining high,*
> *The great North Star with its steady light,*
> *O'er land and sea a beacon bright.*
> *Alaska's flag to Alaskans dear,*
> *The simple flag of a last frontier.*

DID YOU KNOW?

Researchers and historians have recently discovered that Benny Benson was 14 years old when he designed the flag, not 13 as previously thought.

Benny went on to become an airplane mechanic and later moved to Kodiak. He died at the age of 59 of a heart attack.

2

HIGHS, LOWS & OTHER ALASKAN GEOLOGY FACTS

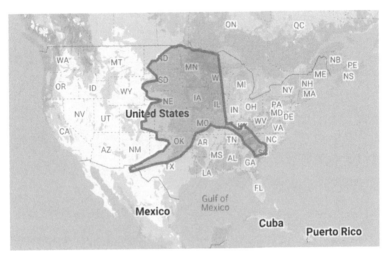

A map of Alaska compared to the contiguous United States - made by thetruesize.com

BIGGEST STATE BY AREA

Alaska is the largest state in the United States. Let's talk numbers to give you a better idea of just how massive Alaska is.

Alaska is about 663,000 square miles (1,717,162 square kilometers) or about 365,000,000 acres. Texas, the second largest US state, is just under 269,000 square miles. Texas would fit into Alaska twice, with room to spare. In fact, if you combined Texas, Montana and California, Alaska would still be bigger.

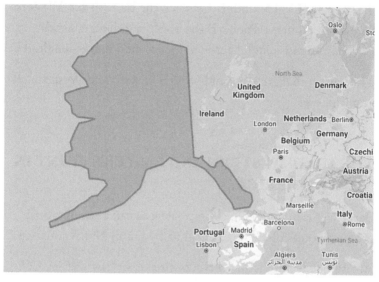

A map of Alaska compared to Europe - made by truesize.com

ALASKA IS HUGE

Alaska is about one-fifth the size of the entire Lower 48 US states. It seems like an understatement to say that Alaska is massive. If Alaska were a separate country, it would be in the top 20 biggest countries in the world.

AREA PER PERSON

Alaska, despite its size, is the third least-populated state in the union. It works out to be about .91 square mile (2.26 square kilometers) per person. Wyoming is the least-populated state in the US, followed by Vermont, then Alaska.

ALASKA IS IN TWO HEMISPHERES

The geographical boundary between the Eastern and Western Hemispheres in the Pacific is the 180th meridian. Alaska's Aleutian Islands extend across the 180° meridian of longitude.

This means that Alaska is in both the Eastern and Western Hemispheres.

THE MOST WESTERN AND EASTERN POINT IN NORTH AMERICA

Because it is in both hemispheres, Alaska can claim the westernmost point AND the easternmost point in North America.

Amatignak Island, with GPS coordinates 51°16'7"N 179°8'55"W, is the westernmost point in all US territories.

Semisopochnoi Island, with GPS coordinates 51°57'42"N 179°46'23"E, is the easternmost point in all US territories.

FARTHER WEST THAN THE HAWAIIAN ISLANDS

One of the outer Aleutian Islands, a tiny, uninhabited island called Semisopochnoi Island, is the westernmost point of land in Alaska, the United States and North America.

· · ·

It's farther west than the Hawaiian Islands. But again, it's so far west, it's actually east, because it's on the opposite side of the 180th meridian and therefore in the Eastern Hemisphere.

ALASKA'S MOST WESTERN POINT ON THE MAINLAND

If we're talking on the mainland, then Alaska's most western point is on the Seward Peninsula. From its most western point, at Cape Prince of Wales on the Bering Strait, the Russia-US sea boundary is only 15 miles (8.05 km) away, and Siberia is only about 55 miles (88.5 km) away.

MOST NORTHERN POINT

The northernmost point of Alaska and of the United States is Point Barrow, on the Arctic coast. Point Barrow, however, is not the northernmost point on the North American mainland. That distinction belongs to Canada, at Murchison Promontory, which lies 40 miles or 64 km farther north.

THE UNITED STATES' MOST NORTHERN, EASTERN AND WESTERN POINTS ARE ALL FOUND IN ALASKA

With Point Barrow being the farthest north, and the Aleutian Islands covering both the easternmost and westernmost points, Alaska can claim to be the US state with the most northern, eastern and western points.

· · ·

SOUTHERNMOST POINT OF ALASKA

The tip of Amatignak Island, in the Aleutian Island chain, is not only the most westerly longitude point, but also the southernmost point.

CLOSER TO RUSSIA THAN TO THE REST OF THE UNITED STATES

From the mainland of Alaska, the shortest distance between Alaska and Russia is only 55 miles (88.5 km), separated only by the Bering Strait.

But between two islands located in the Bering Strait, less than three miles of water separate Russia and the United States. These two islands are Big Diomede and Little Diomede. Russia owns Big Diomede and the US owns Little Diomede.

Map of Alaska via Depositphotos.com

The International Date Line separates the two islands, which means these two islands lie in two different hemispheres and are marking two different days. Big Diomede is 21 hours ahead of Little Diomede.

ON A CLEAR DAY, YOU CAN SEE RUSSIA FROM ALASKA

Depending on the weather and where you stand, you can stand on Little Diomede and see Big Diomede, since they are less than three miles apart. On the mainland, in the westernmost city of Alaska, Wales, it is possible to spot the Siberian mountains in Russia.

ALASKA-CANADA BORDER

The shared border between Alaska and Canada is more than 1,538 miles or 2,475 km long.

HIGHEST POINT

The highest point in Alaska is at the summit of North America's tallest mountain, Denali, which for a time was known as Mount McKinley. It rises 20,310 feet, or 6,190 meters, above sea level.

The Indigenous people of that area, the Koyukon Athabaskans, long ago gave the peak the name of Dinale, or Denali, which means "high" or "tall."

. . .

LARGEST ISLAND

Of the 2,670 named islands of Alaska, Kodiak, in the Gulf of Alaska, is the largest, with 3,588 square miles, or 9,293 square kilometers. It is the second largest island in the US, after Hawaii's Big Island.

SMALLEST ISLAND

With an area of just two square miles or 5.18 square kilometers, Little Diomede Island, just over two miles or 3.2 kilometers to the east of Big Diomede Island, Russia, is Alaska's smallest island.

MORE ISLANDS THAN ANY OTHER US STATE

Alaska has 2,670 named islands, and who knows how many unnamed islands. Big and small, they all help make Alaska the largest state. Florida comes in second place for number of islands.

MORE COASTLINE THAN ALL OF THE US COMBINED

Not to brag or anything, but Alaska has more coastline than any other state. Alaska's coastline measures 6,640 miles (10,686 km) when you look just at the mainland. Florida comes in second for coastline, but with only 1,350 miles (2,173 km).

. . .

When you include Alaska's islands, the total is a whopping 33,904 miles (54,563 km) of coast and shoreline.

COASTLINES ON THREE DIFFERENT SEAS

Not only does Alaska have the most coastline of any US state, but these coasts are on three different seas: the Arctic Ocean, Pacific Ocean and the Bering Sea.

DID YOU KNOW?
Alaska is almost as close to Tokyo (3,520 miles, or 5665 km) as it is to New York City (3,280 miles, or 5,279 km).

Regions of Alaska

SOUTHEAST ALASKA, AKA THE INSIDE PASSAGE

Southeast Alaska, or the Inside Passage region, is a coastal area stretching over 500 miles (805 km) from Ketchikan to Yakutat, known for its forested islands, wildlife such as whales, sea otters and bears. It has Indigenous communities whose rich cultural traditions include totem poles and other types of artwork.

The region's economy thrives on fishing, tourism, and timber, with major cities such as Ketchikan, Sitka, and Juneau serving as its hub. The area is a favorite stop for the cruise ships that bring many visitors to the area each year.

SOUTHCENTRAL ALASKA

Southcentral Alaska is a region that stretches from the Kenai Peninsula to the Matanuska-Susitna Valley, including Anchorage, Alaska's largest city. The area boasts stunning scenery, such as glaciers, mountains, and volcanoes, including North America's highest peak, Denali. Visitors can enjoy outdoor activities like hiking, fishing, and skiing in parks and wilderness areas such as Kenai Fjords National Park and Chugach State Park.

The region has a diverse economy, including the oil and gas industry, tourism, fishing, and transportation. Southcentral Alaska is also home to many small communities with unique cultural and historical attractions, such as the Russian Orthodox Church in Kenai and the Alaska Native Heritage Center in Anchorage.

THE INTERIOR

The Interior is a region that includes large parts of the state's central and eastern sections. It is dominated by vast areas of wilderness, including Denali National Park, the largest national park in the United States.

The region is known for its extreme weather, with long, harsh winters and short, intense summers. The landscape is characterized by rolling hills, vast forests, and countless rivers and lakes. The region is also home to a number of Indigenous communities, including the Athabascan people, who have lived in the region for thousands of years.

ALASKA'S ARCTIC, AKA THE FAR NORTH

The Arctic region of Alaska is in the northernmost part of the state, known for its tundra landscapes and a harsh climate. Indigenous communities such as the Inupiat and Gwich'in have lived there for thousands of years and still practice traditional hunting and fishing. The area is also home to a variety of wildlife, including polar bears and caribou, and the Arctic National Wildlife Refuge.

Despite being a significant site of oil and gas production, the region is remote and has limited infrastructure, making it a challenging environment to live and work in.

SOUTHWEST ALASKA

Southwest Alaska is a sparsely populated region that includes the Alaska Peninsula and the Aleutian Islands, with diverse Alaska Native cultures such as the Aleut, Alutiiq, and Yup'ik peoples. It has rugged terrain, active volcanoes, and abundant wildlife such as brown bears, caribou, and sea otters.

The commercial fishing industry is vital, with salmon and crab being the most significant catches. The region has national wildlife refuges such as the Alaska Maritime National Wildlife

Refuge and Izembek National Wildlife Refuge. The city of Kodiak on Kodiak Island is the region's largest community and serves as a transportation and commerce hub.

WESTERN ALASKA

Western Alaska includes the Seward Peninsula and Yukon-Kuskokwim Delta. It has small communities with a great cultural heritage, including the Yup'ik, Cup'ik, and Inupiaq peoples. It encompasses tundra, hills, and coastlines, populated by caribou, muskox and many bird species. Fishing, hunting, and other subsistence activities are important for the economy and way of life.

3

CRAZY ALASKAN WEATHER

THIS ALASKA TOWN HAS THE LONGEST AND SHORTEST DAYS IN THE US

The most northernmost town in the US is called Utqiaġvik. The village was known for a time as Barrow, but reverted to its traditional Inupiag name in 2016 when residents voted to change it. In the Inupiaq language, Utqiaġvik means "the place where we hunt snowy owls."

Its extreme northern location means it gets 24 hours of daylight, also known as polar day, during the summer months. This usually starts around May 10th and goes to August 2nd. The 24 hours of daylight usually lasts around 82 days, but can vary from year to year.

A similar thing happens during the winter, except instead of 24 hours of daylight, its 24 hours of darkness, which is referred to as a polar night. This usually starts around November 18th and lasts till around January 23rd. While the sun does not come over the horizon during that time, there is some degree of twilight.

LAND OF THE MIDNIGHT SUN

Given that there may be full days and even months of the sun not setting, depending on where you happen to be in the state, it's no wonder Alaska is called the "Land of the Midnight Sun."

MIDNIGHT SUN BASEBALL GAME

For more than 100 years, the Midnight Sun Baseball Game has been played on every Summer Solstice in Fairbanks. It's hosted by the Alaska Goldpanners, and local and hardcore baseball fans from around the world pack into Growden Memorial Park for this unique game.

The game goes the standard nine innings, but the first pitch is thrown at 10:30 p.m. Because of the midnight sun, no artificial lighting is allowed or needed to light up the field.

Instead of singing "Take Me Out to the Ballgame" the enthusiastic crowd sings "Alaska's Flag" at midnight.

HOT, BUT NOT THAT HOT

The hottest temperature ever recorded in Alaska was 100°F (37.8°C) in Fort Yukon in 1915. The only time that record came close to being broken was in June 1969, when it got to a toasty 98°F (36.7°C) at Richardson.

DID YOU KNOW?

Alaska has never recorded high temperatures above 100 degrees Fahrenheit (37.8°C).

COLDEST TEMPERATURES RECORDED IN THE US

The lowest temperature ever recorded in Alaska and in the US was a painfully cold -80°F (-62°C) at Prospect Creek Camp on January 23, 1971. That's almost as cold as the average temperature on the surface of Mars. Temperatures on Mars average about -81°F (-62°C).

ALASKA'S AVERAGE WEATHER

Alaska is such a large place, and the weather varies greatly depending on where you are in the state. Winters in Alaska are long, icy, snowy and dark, while the summers are cool and partly cloudy. During the summer, average daytime temperatures throughout the state range from the mid-50s to the 90s Fahrenheit (12 to 35°C). Alaska is tied with Hawaii as the state with the lowest record high temperature in the US. During the winter, average temperatures range from the 10s°F to mid-20s°F (-12 to -4°C).

. . .

WHEN IT RAINS, IT POURS...ESPECIALLY IN SITKA

Some parts of Alaska get quite a bit of rain. Sitka is the second wettest city in the US, with its average of 173 rainy days a year (that's about 47 percent of the year). The number 1 wettest city in the US is Hilo, Hawaii, which receives 211 days of rain each year, on average.

SOUTHEAST ALASKA IS A RAINFOREST

Not all of Alaska is cold and snowy. Southeast Alaska is home to the Tongass National Forest, which is considered the largest temperate rainforest in the world. The city of Ketchikan, Alaska which is within the area of Tongass National Forest, averages 140 to 160 inches of rain per year with 234 days of some type of precipitation.

HOLY SNOW!

In the winter of 1952–1953, a record-breaking 974.1 inches (2474.2 cm) or 81.1 feet (24.7 m) of snow fell on Thompson Pass near the town of Valdez. This is the most snow ever recorded in one season in Alaska and in the US at the time.

SNOWIEST TOWN IN THE US

305 miles (490 km) east of Anchorage lies the beautiful coastal city of Valdez, also known as Alaska's "little Switzerland." On average, Valdez gets 325 inches (826 cm) of snow every year.

That's over 27 feet (8.2 m) of snow. This makes Valdez not only the snowiest town in Alaska, but the snowiest town in the US.

To put this in perspective, one of the snowiest mountain ski resorts, Alta ski resort in Utah, gets an average of 458.3 inches (1164.1 cm) per year. That adds up to over 38 feet (11.6 m). The snowiest major city in the US is Rochester, New York, with 102 inches (259.1 cm) of snow per year. That's over 8 feet (2.4 m).

REPUTATION FOR BEING COLD IS VALID

Since nearly one-third of Alaska lies within the Arctic Circle, it makes sense that it would have a reputation for being cold. Much of Alaska is built on a layer of permafrost, which is permanently frozen soil lying below a surface layer that thaws in summer.

ALASKA'S TUNDRA

Much of Alaska is also made up of tundra landscapes, which are flat, vast and treeless Arctic plains with whipping winds. Tundra comes from the Finnish word tunturi, which means "treeless heights."

ALMOST NO SNOW DAYS

Even with all the snow that Alaska gets and the butt-clenching cold temperatures that seem the norm, schools rarely have snow days. Kids enjoy outdoor recess in the cold and snow, and they're only kept inside when it reaches -10°F (-23°C) or below.

___

4

ALASKA'S WILD & RUGGED NATURE

ALASKA IS 14.2% WATER

With more than 3 million lakes and over 12,000 rivers, it's easy to see how 14.2 percent of Alaska is water. That works out to be 94,743 square miles (245,383 km) of water area.

ALASKA HAS OVER 3 MILLION LAKES

Geez, I wouldn't have wanted to be the person to count all of them. Alaska's figure of 3 million lakes counts only bodies of water bigger than five acres, so that number doesn't include all of the ponds. Only about 3,197 of the lakes have official names.

With all of this water, it should come as no surprise that Alaska is home more than 40 percent of the surface water resources in the whole US. No wonder Alaska is so boat-friendly and has so many seaplanes.

. . .

ALASKA'S LARGEST LAKES

Alaska's largest lakes include Iliamna Lake, Lake Clark, Naknek Lake, Becharof Lake, Selawik Lake, Tusteumena Lake and Kenai Lake.

RIVERS DEFINITELY RUN THROUGH IT

According to Alaska's Department of Fish and Game, Alaska has more than 12,000 rivers, the Yukon being the longest, with 1266 miles (2037 km) in Alaska and the rest flowing through Canada's Yukon Territory for a total of 1980 miles (3190 km). The river runs north before taking a turn to the west through Alaska before emptying into the Bering Sea.

The Yukon River is the third longest river in the US, following the Missouri and the Mississippi.

RIVERS ARE A KEY PART OF ALASKA'S ECONOMY

Rivers are not only important for Alaska's wildlife, but also provide a system of moving goods and people through the state.

HOW MANY GLACIERS???

Maybe because almost one-third of Alaska lies inside the Arctic Circle, about 5 percent of the state is covered in glaciers. The Alaska Almanac estimates there are about 100,000 glaciers in Alaska. That's way too many to name!

. . .

According to the Geographic Names Information System, there are roughly 664 named glaciers in Alaska.

Hubbard Glacier in Alaska. Photo by Peter Hansen on Unsplash.

In Glacier Bay National Park alone, there are roughly 1,000 glaciers. The park's website says that, unfortunately, because of climate change, 95 percent of Alaska's glaciers are thinning, stagnating or retreating, so there may be fewer of them in decades to come.

DID YOU KNOW?

Glaciers are Alaska's number one tourist attraction. About 5 percent of Alaska is glacierized, including 11 mountain ranges, 1 large island, an island chain, and 1 archipelago.

ALASKA HAS NORTH AMERICA'S LARGEST GLACIER

The largest glacier in Alaska is the Bering Glacier complex, which, combined with the Bagley Icefield, covers about about 1900 square miles (5200 square kilometers).

ICE WORMS AND ALASKAN GLACIERS

Ice worms are small, dark-colored worms that live on glaciers in coastal mountains of Alaska, British Columbia, Washington, Oregon, and California. They move through the ice using hair-like setae on their bodies and generate their own body heat to survive in sub-zero temperatures. Although not harmful to humans, they can be a nuisance to climbers and hikers as they tend to crawl onto clothing and gear, and their bodies release a foul odor when they die.

ALASKA HAS THE TWO LARGEST FORESTS IN THE US

Alaska has not one, but two of the largest forests in the nation. The largest is called Tongass and is in the southeast of Alaska near Juneau, the capital. Tongass National Forest covers 16.7 million acres, and most of it has a temperate rainforest climate. At 16.7 million acres, Tongass National Forest is just a bit bigger than the state of West Virginia, with 15.5 million acres.

Wildlife you'd see in Tongass include eagles, bears, salmon, wolves, otters, swans, and Sitka Blacktail Deer which are much smaller than the Mule Deer and White Tail deer of the Lower 48.

Alaska's second largest forest is the Chugach National Forest, in Southcentral Alaska. Chugach has 4.8 million acres and is a little smaller than the state of New Jersey.

SHAKE, SHAKE, SHAKE ... ALASKA'S EARTHQUAKES

To say that Alaska is seismically active is an understatement. The Alaska Earthquake Center reported more than 150,000 earthquakes in the past five years, 31 of those have a magnitude of six or higher on the Richter scale.

Of the ten strongest earthquakes ever recorded in the world, three have shaken things up in Alaska. Now, while these stats seem scary, it's worth noting that many of these earthquakes have happened in uninhabited areas or are so small they are barely felt.

. . .

THE SECOND STRONGEST EARTHQUAKE EVER HAPPENED IN ALASKA

Fourth Avenue in downtown Anchorage, Alaska after the 1964 Alaska Earthquake. Photo by U.S. Army, Public domain, via Wikimedia Commons

A 9.2 magnitude earthquake rocked central Alaska on Good Friday, March 27, 1964. It lasted for four minutes and thirty-eight seconds, but 52 separate aftershocks shook the area over the next three days, 11 of which measured higher than 6.0 on the Richter scale. Two hundred miles southwest of Anchorage, areas near Kodiak were permanently raised by 30 feet (9m). Other areas dropped as much as 8 feet (2.4m). People as far away as Texas and Florida reported movement directly related to the earthquake, such as seeing their "pool jiggle."

. . .

Miraculously, only nine people died in Anchorage and 115 throughout the rest of the state.

The strongest recorded earthquake in the world happened only four years earlier in Chile, with a magnitude of 9.5.

DID YOU KNOW?

In 1967, Anchorage established the 134-acre 'Earthquake Park' in memory of earthquake victims. The park showcases a seismograph, a fault line model linked to the quake, and a timeline depicting Alaska's seismic past.

ALASKA IS HOME TO 17 OF NORTH AMERICA'S TALLEST MOUNTAINS

Of the 20 highest peaks in the North America, 17 are in Alaska, including the number 1 highest peak, Denali, at 20,310 feet (6,190 m) above sea level. A few other high peaks include: Mount Saint Elias (18,009 ft or 5,489 m), Mount Foraker (17,257 ft or 5,230 m), Mount Bona (16,550 ft or 5,044 m), Mount Blackburn (16,390 ft or 4,996 m) and Mount Sandford (17,237 ft or 4,949 m).

THE LAND OF VOLCANOES

Where there are earthquakes, there are often volcanoes. Alaska has often been referred to as the "land of volcanoes," since it has more than 130 volcanoes, of which 90 are considered active, having erupted within the past ten thousand years. Only half of those have been active since 1760. The most active volcanoes are in the Wrangell Mountains and Aleutian Islands.

But don't worry; according to the US Geological Survey, Alaskan volcanoes have produced only one or two eruptions since 1900. The most recent violent eruption happened in 1912, when Novarupta Volcano erupted and created the Valley of Ten Thousand Smokes, now part of Katmai National Park.

———

Alaska's National & State Parks

ALASKA HAS EIGHT NATIONAL PARKS

Alaska's eight national parks make up two-thirds of the land administered by the entire National Park System—roughly 54 million acres in all.

ONLY THREE OF ALASKA'S EIGHT NATIONAL PARKS ARE ACCESSIBLE BY ROAD

Visitors can travel by road only to Denali, Kenai Fjords and Wrangell St. Elias national parks. The other five are accessible only by boat or air.

. . .

ALASKA HAS THE ONLY ARCTIC NATIONAL PARKS, MONUMENTS & PRESERVES IN THE US

Four of the eight national parks in Alaska lie entirely north of the Arctic Circle. These four arctic parks include Cape Krusenstern National Monument, Gates of the Arctic National Park and Preserve, Kobuk Valley National Park, and Noatak National Preserve.

GATES OF THE ARCTIC NATIONAL PARK & PRESERVE

Gates of the Arctic National Park is above the Arctic Circle, one of the wildest, most rugged and remote places on the continent. There is not one single paved road or trail. During the Arctic summer, days are long because the sun doesn't set for weeks, and during the Arctic winter, the only lights are those of the moon and Aurora Borealis.

Gates of the Arctic National Park is about four times larger than Yellowstone National Park. Here you'll find glaciated valleys, scenic rivers and arctic tundra, along with the northernmost mountain range, the Brooks Range. Boreal Mountain and Frigid Crags, two massive peaks, stand on opposite sides of the north fork of the Koyukuk River and form the "gates" that inspired the park's name.

NOATAK NATIONAL PRESERVE

In Noatak National Preserve, you will find Alaska's largest caribou herd, known as the Western Arctic herd, with more than 200,000 caribou. They migrate north each spring and south each fall across the tundra. Noatak National Preserve borders Gates of the Arctic on the west and protects the largest untouched, mountain-ringed river basin in the US. It's also home to the wild Noatak River, one of the longest undammed rivers in North America.

KOBUK VALLEY NATIONAL PARK

Kobuk Valley National Park sits just south of Noatak between two mountain ranges: the Baird Mountains on the north and the Waring Mountains to the south. The scenic Kobuk River flows for 61 miles (98 km) along the southern end of the park. This river is popular with visitors, who love to float down the river in the warmer months.

DID YOU KNOW?
An Arctic National Park with Sand Dunes?
Sand dunes in the Arctic? Heck yes! At least when you visit Kobuk Valley National Park. Here you will find sand dunes 10 stories high that make you think you're in the desert and not the Arctic. These sand dunes happen to be the largest in the Arctic.

CAPE KRUSENSTERN NATIONAL MONUMENT

Cape Krusenstern is known for its spectacular scenery, including rolling hills, wildflowers, and coastal lagoons. It borders the Chukchi Sea and Kotzebue Sound and is west of the three other parks: Kobuk Valley, Noatak and Gates of the Arctic.

Cape Krusenstern preserves more than 5,000 years' worth of prehistoric and historic Alaska Native artifacts. Here you'll find campsites, house ruins, stone tools, pottery, burial grounds and hunting and whaling tools.

The monument covers over 650,000 acres and has a rich history, including being the location of the first contact between Europeans and the Inupiaq people in the late 18th century.

SEVEN OF THE TEN LARGEST NATIONAL PARKS ARE IN ALASKA

Alaska just seems to go big, so are you even surprised to learn that seven of the ten biggest national parks are found in Alaska? I didn't think so.

THE LARGEST NATIONAL PARK IN THE US

Alaska's Wrangell-St. Elias National Park is massive. To put it into perspective, it's roughly the same size as Yellowstone National Park, Yosemite National Park and Switzerland combined. Or if that's too hard to visualize, it's equal to six Yellowstones.

Not only is it the largest national park in the US, but also the most diverse. It's got everything from temperate rainforest to frigid tundra. Four major mountain ranges meet together within the park to create a tangle of 18,000-foot (5,486 m) peaks, which include nine of the 16 highest peaks in the US. Oh, and it's got several massive glaciers (one larger than the state of Rhode Island) and spectacular, deep river valleys.

ONE OF ALASKA'S BEST KEPT SECRETS

The Nabesna Glacier, found inside Wrangell-St. Elias National Park, is the world's longest interior valley glacier and the longest valley glacier in North America. It covers an area of over 200 square miles (518 square km), and is over 50 miles (80 km) long. Despite its size and location, Nabesna Glacier is relatively unknown and attracts far fewer visitors than some of the more popular destinations in Alaska.

WORLD'S LARGEST INTERNATIONAL PROTECTED WILDERNESS

Wrangell-St. Elias National Park is designated as a UNESCO World Heritage Site. While it's not the largest World Heritage Site, it is the world's largest internationally protected wilderness.

DENALI NATIONAL PARK

Denali National Park, formerly known as Mount McKinley National Park, centers on the highest mountain in North America, Denali (highest point at 20,310 ft or 6,190 m). Denali National Park is one of the three parks in Alaska that you can get to by car. It's 240 miles (386 km) by road from Anchorage and 125 miles (201 km) from Fairbanks. The park has just one road, called the Denali Park Road. The road is 92 miles (148 km) long, and only the first 15 miles (24 km) are paved.

Bull caribou walking in front of Denali.

Denali National Park is 9,492 square miles (24,584 square km). To compare, New Hampshire is 9,351 square miles (24,218 square km) in area and Massachusetts is 10,555 square miles (27337 square km).

DENALI THE ONLY NATIONAL PARK WITH WORKING SLED DOGS

Denali National Park has had sled dogs working with rangers since 1922; 2022 marked 100 years of this practice. In such a remote area with extreme weather, having reliable transportation is the difference between life and death. At 40 below zero (in both Fahrenheit and Celsius), motors may refuse to start. Snowmobiles can get bogged down and sink. Sled dogs are always enthusiastic and ready to go, whether on patrol or to haul heavy materials.

. . .

Denali sled dogs retire at the age of nine with more than 8,000 miles (12,875 km) under their harnesses and can be adopted by the right people. An application form can be found on the Denali National Park website.

DID YOU KNOW?

Denali National Park was created in 1917 for one main reason: to protect the Dall sheep, which was being poached at alarming rates. Eventually, Congress expanded the park boundaries and added to the list of things the park was meant to protect, including the tallest mountain in the US.

GLACIER BAY

At last count there were 1,045 glaciers in the park, which cover 27 percent, or 2,055 square miles (5,322 square km) of the park. There are more than 50 named glaciers, seven of which calve icebergs into the sea.

Along with Wrangell-St. Elias National Park, Glacier Bay is also a designated UNESCO World Heritage Site.

About 80 percent of visitors to Glacier Bay see it from cruise ships and tour boats. National Park Service rangers often go aboard the ships to talk about Glacier Bay and its many unique characteristics.

DID YOU KNOW?

Some humpback whales spend the summer in Glacier Bay and swim to Hawaii for the winter.

KENAI FJORDS NATIONAL PARK

Kenai Fjords is where mountains, ice and ocean meet. It was established to protect the Harding Icefield and all of its glaciers, coastal fjords and islands, and the animals that call it home. The Harding Icefield is the largest feature here, covering half the park. It's about 50 miles (80 km) across at its longest point and 20 miles (32 km) wide at its widest point. At least 28 glaciers flow from the Harding Icefield.

Volcanoes, Salmon and Bears, Oh My!

KATMAI NATIONAL PARK AND PRESERVE

Katmai is a national park famous for its brown bears (a species also known as grizzlies, when they live inland). It has more bears than people! An estimated 2,200 brown bears live in the park. One of the best places to see bears is at Brooks Camp, where they catch salmon in the Brooks River. You can only get to Katmai by air or boat, because there are no roads.

Bears fishing for salmon in the Brooks River in Katmai National Park and Preserve. Photo by Pradeep Nayak on Unsplash.

The park also has volcanoes, including Mount Katmai, which erupted in 1917 and created the Valley of Ten Thousand Smokes. Bear watching is the most popular activity, and July is the busiest month. Other activities include hiking, camping, skiing, and kayaking.

LIVE BEAR CAM AT KATMAI NATIONAL PARK

During the summer, Katmai National Park turns on their live web cam at Brooks River. Here you can watch the bears feast on salmon, spot a bald eagle or two, and even the occasional wolf trying to get in on the salmon action. Bears have been known to catch more than 30 salmon per day during the peak season in late June and July.

Watch it here: https://bit.ly/Katmai-Bear-Cam

. . .

FAT BEAR WEEK

A contest that started in October 2014, when park rangers invited visitors to vote on which bear was the fattest. It was a hit, and the contest went digital when the park put up a single elimination tournament bracket on Facebook.

Every October, when the brown bears of Katmai are at their fattest, the park presents photographs of two bears, asking people around the world to vote on which they think is the fattest. The one with the most likes moves on in the competition, until the winner is crowned on Fat Bear Tuesday the following week. A total of 12 bears become part of the voting.

Bears fatten up by eating salmon along the Brooks River to prepare for the long winter hibernation. They must survive on their fat stores for six months, so it's important they fatten up. An adult male bear normally weighs between 700 and 900 pounds (317 and 408 kg) in mid-summer and, after fattening up, can often weigh over 1,200 pounds (544 kg) by late summer and fall.

The contest is all about raising awareness of the bears, helping the public understand how bears survive, why they survive, and what they need to survive, and to celebrate the ecosystem at Katmai that supports all of this.

DID YOU KNOW?

THE YO-YO BEAR DIET

Bears lose up to a third of their body weight during hibernation. From July to September, adult males pack on an impressive 400-500 pounds (180-225 kg) in a couple of months, eating big fat salmon.

LAKE CLARK

Lake Clark is one of the most remote national parks in the US. The park protects rainforests, alpine tundra, glaciers, glacial lakes, salmon-bearing rivers and two volcanoes (Mount Redoubt and Mount Iliamna). Mount Redoubt's most recent eruptions were in 1989 and 2009, so it is definitely considered an active volcano.

In Alaska, where there are salmon, there are usually brown bears, and Lake Clark National Park has plenty of both. Bear watching is a common activity for visitors.

No roads lead to Lake Clark, so it's all about boat and air travel to this picturesque park. In the summer, floatplanes are most often used. In the winter, bush planes can land with wheels, skis or wheeled-skis, depending on snow and ice conditions.

The Northern Lights

Alaska, especially in the city of Fairbanks, often sees the
Northern Lights, also known as the Aurora Borealis. The
Northern Lights are bands and waves of brightly colored light
that dance and move across the night sky, most often visible
between mid-August and mid-April.

Northern Lights seen in Alaska. Photo by Pixabay

WHAT ARE THE NORTHERN LIGHTS?

The Aurora Borealis is a natural light show caused by charged
particles from the sun slamming into gases in Earth's
atmosphere, producing flashes of light.

The Earth's magnetic field redirects these particles towards the
north (Northern Lights) and south poles (Southern Lights),

creating stunning light displays that are best seen when closer to the poles.

The colors seen depend on the energy level of each solar particle and which particle it collides with in Earth's upper atmosphere.

Auroras often start with a green glow, but other colors that can be seen include shades of green, red, yellow, purple, and blue.

HOW AND WHEN TO SEE THE NORTHERN LIGHTS IN ALASKA

While the Northern Lights are unpredictable, we do have an idea of the best times of year to see them and the types of conditions that make seeing them most likely.

The best months to see them in Alaska are the darker months between mid-August and mid-April, with March and September being particularly good.

The skies must be clear and dark. It's best to start looking about an hour and half after the sun sets, with peak activity falling between the winter hours of 11:30 p.m. and 3:30 a.m., around 1:30 a.m. being the best.

. . .

The brilliance of the display depends on the degree of solar activity; some years are better than others.

DID YOU KNOW?

There are Northern Lights, but there are also Southern Lights. The Northern Lights are called the Aurora Borealis (dawn of the north) while the Southern Lights are known as Aurora Australis (dawn of the south). To the Romans, Aurora was the goddess of the morning.

5

ALASKA'S WILDLIFE & ANIMAL FACTS

MOOSE, BEARS, WHALES, OH MY!

Alaska is home to a wide variety of animals and wildlife. When most people think of Alaska, they think of moose, bears, salmon, whales and polar bears. But you'd also find wolves, lynx, muskox, bison, caribou, puffins, seals, and wolverines.

Alaska's State Animals

ALASKA'S STATE FISH: GIANT KING SALMON

Alaska has 48 species of fish and five types of salmon, but the official state fish is the Giant King Salmon, also known as Chinook. The Chinook salmon is the largest of the Pacific salmon, typically measuring about 36 inches in length and often well over 30 pounds (13.6 kg). The record is 126 pounds (57 kg). Now, that's a big fish!

. . .

ALASKA STATE MARINE MAMMAL: BOWHEAD WHALE

Bowhead whales get their name from the shape of their upper jaw, which arches upward, producing a bow-shaped head. They have the largest mouth and head in the animal kingdom; it takes up about one-third of their body. They are the most well-adapted whales when it comes to ice and spend most of their life near the ice in the Bering, Chuckchi and Beaufort seas.

ALASKA'S STATE LAND MAMMAL: MOOSE

Adult male moose. Photo by Shivam Kumar on Unsplash

Adult moose range from 800 pounds to 1,600 pounds (362 to 725 kg) and can be just under six feet (1.8 m) tall.

. . .

Humans and moose have similar taste in where they live, preferring low-lying land next to rivers and streams, which naturally makes us unlikely neighbors.

Moose sleep on the ground like deer. They can store over 100 pounds (45 kg) of food in their stomachs at one time; they can move each ear and eye independently; and their home range may be up to 50 square miles (129 square km). A male moose is called a bull, a female moose is a cow, and a baby moose is a calf. Only the males have antlers.

ILLEGAL MOOSE BEHAVIOR

It's important to know that it is against the law to feed moose. Why? Because it's incredibly dangerous.

PEOPLE ARE MORE OFTEN HURT BY MOOSE THAN BY BEARS

More people in Alaska are hurt by moose than by bears. Moose are plentiful in Alaska, with numbers ranging from 175,000 to 200,000. To compare, the human population of Alaska in 2022 was about 733,583. There are about 30,000 brown (grizzly) bears, about 100,000 black bears, and 4,000 to 7,000 polar bears.

MOOSE MEAT

Moose are an important source of food for many Alaskans, and at least 7,000 moose are harvested every year, which works out to be about 3.5 million pounds (1.5 million kg) of moose meat. Moose is most often found as steaks, roasts, hamburger, sausage or stew meat.

Black, Grizzly & Polar – Alaska Has All Three Types of North American Bears

Alaska has so many bears that it works out to one bear for every 21 people. All three species of North American bears—polar, black and grizzly—live and thrive in Alaska. Here are a few fun facts about Alaska's bears.

BEAR BASICS

Three species of bears are native to North America: the American black bear, the grizzly bear (also known as the North American brown bear), and the polar bear.

Bears have a great sense of smell and can use it to find food from far away. Some species, such as the polar bear, can smell prey from more than a mile (1.6 kilometers) away.

Bears are typically solitary animals, although they may gather in groups to feed on a particularly abundant food source.

. . .

Bears are generally considered intelligent animals, and they have been known to use tools, solve problems, and even show empathy toward other bears.

Male bears are called boars, females are called sows, and young bears are cubs.

BEARS NOT ONLY FLOAT, BUT CAN SWIM

Having high fat content and an oily fur coat makes it easy for hefty bears to stay afloat and swim.

GRIZZLY BEARS VS BROWN BEARS

While brown bears and grizzly bears are classified as the same species, there are significant differences, the major ones being size and geography.

Grizzlies are usually smaller than brown bears and tend to live and travel in mostly inland areas such as the Interior and Northern regions of Alaska.

Brown bears, on the other hand, live in Alaska's coastal areas, where their diet is rich in salmon and other fish, which might be why they are larger.

GRIZZLY BEARS

A full-grown Alaska grizzly bear normally weighs between 300 and 800 pounds (136-362 kg) and is about six feet (1.8m) in length, nose to tail, with shoulders about three feet (0.9 m) above the ground.

GRIZZLY BEARS CAN MOVE FAST

How fast? Well, it would be wise to not to try to outrun a grizzly. These bears can move around 25–30 mph (40–48 km/h), especially when something or someone gets between them and their cubs or whatever they might be feasting on for dinner. An average walking pace is about 3 mph or 5 km/h, which is about the same as your usual human walking pace.

KODIAK BROWN BEAR VS GRIZZLY BEARS

So what's a Kodiak brown bear, then, and how is it different from the grizzly and the brown bear? Glad you asked. It comes down to size and location again.

KODIAK BEARS ARE BIG

Kodiak brown bears are the largest subspecies of the brown bear and grizzly clan, weighing up to 1,500 pounds. Kodiak bears are the second largest bear in the world, the first being the polar bear.

Kodiak bears are much bigger than grizzly bears in both size and weight. The average Kodiak bear weighs between 660 and 1,320 pounds (300–600 kg) and has been known to grow to over 1,500 pounds, or 680 kg. It can stand anywhere from eight to 10 feet tall when upright. While on all fours, they often stand around 4 feet 4 inches (133 cm) tall at the shoulders.

IT'S ALL ABOUT LOCATION WHEN IT COMES TO BEARS

The only place you'll find Kodiak brown bears is in the Kodiak Archipelago in Alaska. They live in the forests and mountains on the Kodiak Peninsula. It's estimated that there are roughly 3,500 Kodiak bears total in the world.

Grizzlies are found in other parts of Alaska, Washington, Montana, Idaho and western and northern parts of Canada. It's estimated that there are about 50,000 grizzly bears throughout North America.

KODIAK BEARS COME IN A VARIETY OF COLORS

Kodiak bears come in a range of colors, from blond to orange to a dark brown. Kodiak bears live around 20 to 25 years in the wild.

DID YOU KNOW?

Only one person has been killed by a Kodiak bear in the past 75 years. About once every other year, a bear injures a person.

MORE BROWN BEARS THAN PEOPLE

Admiralty Island is known for having more brown bears than the entire Lower 48 states. And there are more bears than people: roughly 1,600 brown bears, outnumbering the human population almost three to one.

BLACK BEARS

Of the three species of bears in Alaska—brown, polar and black —black bears are the most abundant and spread out throughout Alaska. An estimated 100,000 black bears live in Alaska. Black bears are the smallest of the North American bears. Adults are about 29 inches (73 cm) at the shoulders when on all fours and measure about 60 inches (152 cm) from nose to tail. Adult males normally weigh about 180–200 pounds (81–90 kg).

Black bears aren't always black. They can be jet black, bluish black, brown, cinnamon-colored, and even white, though black is the most common. The bluish-colored bears are called glacier bears and are found in Southeast Alaska.

HOW DO YOU KNOW A BLACK BEAR IS A BLACK BEAR AND NOT A BROWN BEAR?

Black bears are normally smaller and have a straight facial profile, and their claws rarely grow more than 1½ inches (3.8 cm) in length. They will often have a brown muzzle and a patch of white hair on their chest.

. . .

AFRAID OF BEARS?

Black bears are the most common and abundant type of bear in North America and have been recorded in all states except Hawaii.

POLAR BEARS

Young polar bears playing in Northern Alaska. Photo by Hans-Jurgen Mager on Unsplash.

Polar bears are found in Canada, Alaska, Greenland, Russia and Norway. While not all polar bears live in the high Arctic, all polar bears live where there is snow and ice. To spot polar bears in Alaska, you can usually find them near Barrow, now called Utqiagvik, and Kaktovik, between August and October.

. . .

Polar bears have longer necks, narrower heads, shorter claws, bigger feet and smaller ears than other bears. Their white or yellow coat is water-repellent. Their large feet help them swim and walk on thin ice. The bottoms of their feet are nearly covered in fur. They also have excellent night vision, which is important since most of their hunting is done in the dark Arctic winter months, where there is little to no sunlight for months.

POLAR BEARS ARE THE BIGGEST BEARS

Polar bear males can weigh more than 1,700 pounds (771 kg), but the average is around 600–1,200 pounds (272–544 kg) and eight to 10 feet (2.4-3 m) in length. Male polar bears are twice the size of female polar bears.

POLAR BEARS ARE LIKE SHARKS WHEN IT COMES TO SENSE OF SMELL

A polar bear's sense of smell is its superpower. It can smell prey, often a seal, up to 9.9 miles (16 km) away. It can even detect a seal in the water under 3 feet (1 m) of compacted snow.

POLAR BEARS DON'T HIBERNATE

The biggest hunting season for polar bears is during the winter, so this is when they are the most active. They don't have time to hibernate. It's important they eat enough food during the winter to build up enough fat reserves to go several months in the summer without eating anything.

. . .

Pregnant polar bears do make dens in the winter so that they can give birth to their cubs in a sheltered, warm, and safe environment, but they are not hibernating.

POLAR BEARS ARE BLACK AND WHITE – WELL, KIND OF

Polar bears have jet black skin underneath all of that thick fur. Their fur isn't actually white but translucent, with a hollow core that reflects light, which helps them blend in with their surroundings. It only appears white because it's reflecting the visible light.

Their black skin helps them soak up the sun and keep warm. Under their thick fur, they also have a layer of fat, called blubber, that helps insulate them from the freezing temperatures on land and in the water.

POLAR BEARS ARE EXCELLENT SWIMMERS

Polar bears can swim for long distances and steadily for many hours as they navigate from one piece of ice to another. They can stay under water for about two minutes. Not only can they swim for a long time, they swim quickly at speeds up to 6 mph (10 km/h) in the water. They use their large, slightly webbed front paws to paddle while holding their back legs flat like a rudder.

While they can swim well and fairly fast, they aren't quick enough to consistently catch seals in open water. They normally hunt seals on the ice, waiting patiently near seal breathing holes or on the edge of the ice for a seal to come to the surface.

POLAR BEARS LEAVE DNA IN THEIR FOOTPRINTS

Scientists can extract polar bear DNA from their footprints in the snow. Two small scoops of snow from the footprint will reveal not just its DNA, but even the DNA of the seal it had for lunch.

GROLAR BEARS OR PIZZLY BEARS DO EXIST

Half polar bear and half grizzly bear. Photo by Stefan David via Flickr (CC by SA-2.0)

What do you get when you cross a polar bear with a grizzly bear? You guessed it! A grolar bear or pizzly bear, and these polar bear-grizzly bear hybrids do exist! Wild hybrids are usually born from polar bear mothers. Now, while this seems wacky, it might help to know that polar bears did evolve from brown bears.

DID YOU KNOW?

Because they spend most of their lives on the Arctic Ocean Sea ice, Alaska's polar bears are considered a marine mammal and are protected under the Marine Mammal Protection Act.

Alaska's Reindeer & Caribou

REINDEER VS CARIBOU

Reindeer Closeup. Photo by Barry Tan via Pexels.

Alaska has both reindeer and caribou—about 20,000 reindeer and 750,000 caribou. These are the same elk-like species but with a few differences; caribou are larger and undomesticated.

Reindeer were semi-domesticated on the Eurasian continent, so commercial herding is possible.

REINDEER WERE INTRODUCED TO ALASKA

Domesticated reindeer were imported from Siberia and northern Norway in the 1890s by the US government, along with experienced reindeer herders from the Chukchi people of Siberia and the Sámi from northern Norway. The idea was to introduce a new source of meat, hides, milk, and transport to the Native Alaskans. Herding reindeer may also have been meant as a means to "civilize" the Native Alaskans and move them away from their traditional hunting practices and way of life.

ONLY ALASKA NATIVES CAN OWN REINDEER

In 1937, Congress passed the Alaska Reindeer Act, which restricts ownership of reindeer only to the Indigenous people of Alaska. This act is still in place today. According to the University of Alaska Fairbanks, there are currently about 20 reindeer herds and 20,000 reindeer in Western Alaska.

REINDEER WERE ONCE USED TO DELIVER MAIL IN ALASKA

From 1899 to the early 1910s, Alaskan reindeer were used to pull a sleigh and deliver mail to several post office locations in Northwestern Alaska, including several locations above the Arctic Circle.

. . .

REINDEER NOSES ARE INDEED RED

Reindeer have numerous blood vessels in their noses that act as an internal heater and air conditioner, helping to regulate temperature not just in their nose, but in their brain. Using an infrared thermographic camera, you would be able to see that all reindeer have red noses, not just the famous ones named Rudolph.

ALL REINDEER AND CARIBOU HAVE ANTLERS

Caribou and reindeer are the only species in the deer family where both the male and the female have antlers.

The female's antlers are smaller than the males, but they carry them longer. Caribou and reindeer start growing their antlers in the spring. Males lose their antlers in late October/November. Females, especially those who have had babies, don't lose their antlers until May and June. This helps them protect their calves.

DID YOU KNOW?

There are NO penguins in Alaska, except for maybe a few at zoos. Penguins only live natively in the Southern Hemisphere.

Other Notable Alaskan Animals

LYNX – ALASKA'S NATIVE CAT

Similar to a bobcat, but with long legs, furry feet, long tufts at the tip of each ear and a black-tipped short tail, the lynx is the only cat native to Alaska. The lynx is well adapted to living in cold climates and has a thick coat of fur that changes color with the seasons. The lynx has been featured on Alaskan currency, appearing on the back of the 10-cent piece.

BALD EAGLES

There are an estimated 50,000 bald eagles in Alaska, many making their home in Ketchikan, where there are more than 30 nesting sites. Alaska has more bald eagles than all the other US states, combined. Before 2007, bald eagles were on the endangered species list elsewhere, particularly where they had been decimated by pesticides, but they were never deemed endangered in Alaska.

DID YOU KNOW?

Bald eagles make a chirping sound, not the screech that is often dubbed into movies/tv shows.

Bald eagles have a distinctive sound that is often compared to a series of high-pitched whistles or chirps. Their usual call can be described as soft, staccato whistles — a rhythmic kleek kik ik ik ik, somewhat similar to a gull's call. These vocalizations serve as a means of communication among couples and between parents and their young.

Contrary to popular belief, the powerful, piercing cry often associated with eagles in films is not typically the call of a bald eagle. More often than not, that intense scream is attributed to a red-tailed hawk.

ALASKAN GRAY WOLVES

It's worth noting that Alaska has the largest population of gray wolves in the US, an estimated 8,000 to 13,000. Wolves are a protected species in Alaska. Not only are they an important part of the ecosystem; they are also a big draw for tourists from around the world.

MUSKOX

The muskox is not a true ox, but belongs to the family Bovidae, which also includes sheep and goats. Muskox have been around for tens of thousands of years and are native to Alaska, northern Canada, and Greenland. They are well-adapted to the harsh Arctic environment and can survive in temperatures as low as -40 degrees Fahrenheit and Celsius. The fur of the muskox is called qiviut and is highly valued for its warmth and softness. It is traditionally used to make clothing and other items.

HUMPBACK WHALES

Humpbacks are the most commonly seen whale species in Alaska. They are typically found in the waters around Southeast Alaska and Prince William Sound, but can be seen throughout the state. Humpback whales migrate to Alaska in the summer to feed in the nutrient-rich waters before heading back to Hawaii or other warmer waters to breed and give birth during the winter.

Humpback whales are known for their acrobatic displays, including breaching, tail slapping, and spy-hopping (lifting their head out of the water to look around). Humpback whales are known for their songs, which can last up to 20 minutes and can be heard by other whales over long distances.

DID YOU KNOW?

A female humpback whale, nicknamed Phoenix by the locals, is an annual visitor to Ketchikan in the fall.

Phoenix was first seen in Ketchikan in 2017. She is easily recognizable by her distinctive white markings, which give her the appearance of a phoenix rising from the ashes.

Phoenix is estimated to be about 40 years old, and she is believed to have migrated from Hawaii to Alaska. She is one of the few humpback whales who have been documented to make this long journey.

BELUGA WHALES

Beluga whales, also known as white whales, are enchanting marine mammals found in the pristine waters of Alaska. These charming whales are easily recognizable by their distinct white color, bulbous forehead, and sociable nature. In Alaska, beluga whales are primarily found in Cook Inlet, where they form small pods and navigate the frigid waters in search of fish and other prey.

Fun fact: beluga whales are known for their vocal prowess, earning them the nickname "canaries of the sea." They communicate through a variety of clicks, whistles, and songs, which can be heard even above the water's surface.

Additionally, unlike most whales, belugas have a flexible neck that allows them to move their head independently of their body, offering them superior maneuverability while swimming and foraging in the Alaskan waters.

6

ALASKA'S TREES AND PLANTS

ALASKA'S STATE FLOWER: FORGET-ME-NOT

Closeup of forget-me-not flowers, Alaska's state flower. Photo by Anna Rozwadowska on Unsplash.

The alpine forget-me-not flower was chosen as a symbol of Alaska long before it was officially adopted as Alaska's state flower in 1949. The small flowers have five rounded blue petals with a white inner ring and a yellow center. These wild, native perennials grow throughout Alaska's high-altitude meadows and on rocky mountains. They represent one of the few plant families where the blossoms exhibit true blue.

Forget-me-not flowers were part of the inspiration for the blue Alaskan state flag. Benny Benson, the 14-year-old who designed the winning flag design, explained that, "The blue field is for the Alaska sky and the Forget-me-not, an Alaskan flower."

ALASKA'S STATE TREE: SITKA SPRUCE

The Sitka is the largest spruce and one of the largest trees in the world, right up there with redwoods and giant sequoias. Sitka spruce wood is used for a variety of purposes, some of which you wouldn't normally think of: guitars and pianos, because it provides the best tone wood, masts on ships, wooden ship planks, and turbine blades.

FIREWEED

These tall, thin plants produce bright pink and purple blossoms that bloom from the bottom upward. They can cover entire mountainsides and roadside meadows and are a sure sign that summer has arrived in Alaska. When the topmost flower blooms, it's a sign that summer is coming to an end.

Fireweed. Photo by Paul Levesley on Unsplash

Its name comes from the fact that it is one of the first to bloom after a fire sweeps through, and not just in mountains and meadows. After World War II, fireweed was the first plant to blossom in bomb craters in London.

New shoots can be eaten like asparagus. The leaves can be dried and used for tea. Bees feeding on fireweed nectar produce a white honey that tastes great in jams, jellies, and ice cream.

. . .

NO POISON OAK OR POISON IVY

Alaska and Hawaii are the only US states that do not have
poison ivy or poison oak.

COW PARSNIP

Cow parsnip

While hikers in Alaska don't have to worry about poison oak or
poison ivy, they don't get away from annoying, poisonous plants
that easily.

Alaska has what's called cow parsnip, also known as wild
celery. Cow parsnip can grow up between five and 10 feet tall

and has large hollow stems and large, maple-leaf shaped leaves that are divided into three. It has tiny white flowers in flat-topped clusters at the top of each stem.

If you brush up against it, the plant juices (furocoumarins, a photosensitive chemical) can get onto your skin and react with sunlight, causing pain and blistering. If it does get on your skin, wash it off as soon as you can.

People have used cow parsnip stems as straws and even make them into toy pop guns and pipes.

DEVIL'S CLUB

This large spiky shrub is native to the cool, moist forests of the Pacific Northwest, including much of Alaska. The plant is named for its sharp spines, which can cause painful puncture wounds. The spines are also poisonous, and can cause skin irritation, nausea, and vomiting if ingested.

Despite its dangerous spines, devil's club has some medicinal uses. It's harvested and carefully made into salves, chapstick, and lotions and apparently works wonders!

Berries

SALMONBERRY

Salmonberry. Photo by randimal via DepositPhoto.com.

Salmonberries are large, watery, raspberry-like berries and are one of the first wild fruits available each summer. The berries are best in July but are often available mid-June to mid-August. It has been said that an abundance of salmonberries means pink salmon will be plentiful and also foretells an upcoming snowy winter.

LINGONBERRY

These tangy, sweet, and nutritious berries are also called lowbush cranberries, cowberries, red whortleberries or mountain cranberries, and can be found in the Alaskan forests, mountain slopes and even the tundra.

Lingonberry. Photo by blinow61 via DepositPhoto.com.

Lingonberries have more antioxidants than cranberries and have been used for medicinal purposes. Chewing the berries can help a sore throat, relieve an upset stomach or help a headache.

NAGOONBERRY

Sweet, red, raspberry-like fruit that are ripe in mid to late July. They can be eaten fresh or made into jams and jellies.

CLOUDBERRY

Cloudberries are a prized berry in Canada, Russia, Scandinavia, and throughout Alaska. Other names include Nordic berry, bakeapple, low-bush salmonberry and aqpik. A handful of cloudberries contain more vitamin C than a glass of orange juice and any other Alaska berry.

Cloudberry. Photo by blinow61 via DepositPhoto.com.

CROWBERRY

Crowberries are a shiny, dark blue-black or purple berry that are called more often called blackberries or moss berries in Alaska.

They're a sweet and juicy berry which are not only loved by humans, but also by bears and birds. Crowberry bushes are flat and grow close to the ground and are often found on the tundra and alpine slopes of Alaska.

Crowberries are often picked in the autumn after the first, hard frost. The cold makes the berries taste sweeter.

DID YOU KNOW?

The Yup'ik make akutuk or akutaq also known as "Eskimo ice cream," using different berries like cloudberries or crowberries, seal oil, reindeer or caribou fat and sugar. The texture resembles something like buttercream frosting more than regular ice cream.

7

ALASKA'S PEOPLE & POPULATION

ALASKA'S POPULATION

As of 2021, the population of Alaska was over 730,000 people. There are only two U.S. states with smaller populations: Vermont with 650,000, and Wyoming with 580,000.

ALASKAN MEN ARE THE MAJORITY

The majority of Alaskans (52 percent) are men, the highest percentage of all of the US states. A popular saying when it comes to the men goes, "The odds are good, but the goods are odd!"

WHERE MOST ALASKANS LIVE

With roughly 292,500 people, Anchorage is the most populated Alaskan city. Fairbanks ranks number two, with about

33,000 people. Coming in third is the state's capital, Juneau, with 32,000 people.

THE LEAST POPULATED ALASKAN TOWN

With just 21 people, the town of Kupreanof is the smallest Alaskan town.

ROOM TO SPREAD OUT

The population density of Alaska works out to be about 1 to 1.3 people per square mile, the lowest of all US states. The rest of the US averages 87.4 people per square mile. To put it another way, if Manhattan Island, New York, had the same population density as Alaska, only 16 people would be living on the island.

LOW POVERTY RATES

Alaska has a 10.5 percent poverty rate, whereas the rest of the US averages 11.6 percent. Poverty rate is measured in the US by comparing a person's or family's income to a set poverty threshold or minimum amount of income needed to cover basic needs.

Alaska has a higher standard of living and has a higher poverty threshold than the Lower 48 states. The poverty threshold for one person is $16,090 a year. The poverty threshhold for a family of four is $33,130 a year.

. . .

HIGHER THAN AVERAGE MEDIAN HOUSEHOLD INCOME

According to 2022 US census data, the average median income for Alaskans is $80,287, while the rest of the US sits at $70,784. Some 96 percent of households have a computer and 88 percent have internet.

ALMOST EVERYTHING IS SHIPPED OR FLOWN IN

While the average income is higher in Alaska, this evens out because the cost of goods is higher since almost everything has to come long distances. As one example, many communities in Southeast Alaska rely on the twice weekly barge from the port in Seattle for groceries, building supplies, cars, buses, etc. If the weather is bad the barge might not make it in and supplies will be scarce until the next barge arrives.

ALASKA-PROOFING THE KIDS

Children in Alaska are taught survival skills from an early age. As one example, in Ketchikan, the kids have swimming lessons as part of their curriculum in the young elementary grades.

In later elementary grades they have survival training and in 8th grade they do an overnight survival trip to an island with a coffee can of supplies and a tarp. The kids are taught wilderness first aid, how to stay safe from wild animals and which plants and animals are safe to eat and which are harmful or deadly.

. . .

The kids in Southeast Alaska have beach days during low tides to learn about and experience first-hand the things they have been learning.

ALASKANS ARE HAPPY & SELF SUFFICIENT

Alaska is one of the happiest places to live in America. Alaskans tend to have a sense of purpose, strong social and community bonds, and live in a place where exercise and physical activity is almost as common as breathing.

Alaskans are self-sufficient and take care of each other. There is a sense of community that is hard to find elsewhere.

ALASKA MILLIONAIRES

Alaska has its fair share of millionaires. A report in 2020 showed that about 8.18 percent of Alaska's households are millionaires. That works out to roughly 22,300 households.

SLIGHTLY HIGHER LIFE EXPECTANCY

The average life expectancy for Alaskans is 79 years, compared to a US average of 78.8. The state with the highest life expectancy is Hawaii at 82.3, while West Virginia has the lowest at 74.8.

. . .

ALASKA'S ORIGINAL INHABITANTS

At least 14,000 years ago, the first group of human settlers came to what is now known as Alaska. Alaska is home to 229 federally and state-recognized tribes—the largest number in the US. According to the 2021 census, 15.7 percent of the state population identifies as American Indian or Alaska Native, the highest percentage nationwide.

NATIVE CULTURES IN ALASKA

Native Alaska Cultural Groups & Regions

IÑUPIAQ & ST. LAWRENCE ISLAND YUPIK

DENE (Athabascan)

YUP'IK & CUP'IK

EYAK, TLINGIT, HAIDA, & TSIMSHIAN

UNANGAX̂ (ALEUT) & ALUTIIQ/SUGPIAQ

Five Native Alaska Cultural Groups & Regions. Illustration created by the author.

There are 11 distinct Indigenous cultures represented in Alaska: Athabascan, Tlingit, Haida, Tsimshian, Unangax̂ (Aleut), Alutiiq (Sugpiaq), Yup'ik, Cup'ik, Siberian Yupik, Inupiaq, and St. Lawrence Island Yupik.

. . .

These Alaska Native cultures are commonly divided into five groups by region:

- The Eyak, Tlingit, Haida, and Tsimshian peoples of Southeastern Alaska;
- The Inupiaq and St. Lawrence Island Yupik of Northern Alaska and Northwestern Arctic region;
- The Yup'ik and Cup'ik of Southwest Alaska;
- The Athabascan peoples in Southcentral and Interior Alaska;
- The Alutiiq (Sugpiaq) and Unangax̂ peoples of Southcentral Alaska and the Aleutian Islands.

---

1. **Aleut / Unangax̂** (Aleut pronounced uh-LOOT and Unangax̂ pronounced oo-nuh-gash): The Indigenous people of the Aleutian Islands and surrounding areas refer to themselves by two names: Unangax̂, which is their name in their language, and Aleut, the name Russian fur traders gave them. The word Aleut means "coastal dweller" and comes from a Siberian Native language. They have a rich tradition of hunting, fishing, and crafting, and are known for their skill in working with sea otter fur and bird feathers.

2. **Alutiiq / Sugpiaq** (Alutiiq is pronounced a-loo-teek, and Sugpiaq is pronounced soog-pee-ak): The Alutiiq people are indigenous to the Kodiak Archipelago and surrounding regions. They have a long history of maritime subsistence, and are known

for their expertise in kayaking, hunting sea mammals, and fishing.

3. **Iñupiaq** (pronounced ee-NOO-pee-ak): The Iñupiaq people live in the northernmost regions of Alaska, including the North Slope and the Seward Peninsula. They have a deep connection to the land and sea, and are known for their skill in hunting and processing marine mammals like bowhead whales and walruses.

4. **Yup'ik** (pronounced yoo-pik): The Yup'ik people live in Southwestern Alaska, along the coast and the Yukon and Kuskokwim rivers. They have a long tradition of fishing, hunting, and gathering, and are known for their expertise in building and using kayaks. Elders are recognized as leaders in their communities and offer guidance and advice.

5. **Cup'ik** (pronounced choo-pick): The Cup'ik people are a subgroup of the Yup'ik who live in the coastal region around the village of Chevak.

6. **Siberian Yupik / St. Lawrence Island Yupik**: The Siberian Yupik people are a subgroup of the Yupik who live in the villages of Gambell and Savoonga on St. Lawrence Island. They have a rich cultural heritage and are known for their traditional dances, songs, and storytelling. They traditionally hunted whales by harpooning them from small covered canoes called umiaks.

7. **Tlingit** (pronounced CLINK-it): The Tlingit people are indigenous to the southeastern region of Alaska, including the Inside Passage and Glacier Bay. They have a long history of fishing, hunting, and trading,

and are known for their artistic traditions, including totem pole carving and Chilkat weaving.

8. **Haida** (pronounced HIGH-duh): The Haida people live in the southernmost region of Alaska and on Prince of Wales Island, as well as Haida Gwaii and other parts of neighboring British Columbia. They have a rich cultural heritage and are known for their art, including totem poles and intricately carved wooden boxes.

9. **Tsimshian** (pronounced sim-shee-an): The Tsimshian people are indigenous to the region around Prince Rupert, British Columbia, as well as the southernmost part of Alaska. They have a long tradition of fishing, hunting, and trading, and are known for their intricate artwork, including masks and regalia.

10. **Eyak** (pronounced EE-yak): The Eyak people are indigenous to the region around the Copper River and Prince William Sound. The Eyak language is now extinct, but the Eyak people continue to work to preserve their cultural heritage.

11. **Athabascan** (pronounced ATH-uh-BAS-kin): Also called Dene (pronounced DEN-eh). There are 11 distinct subgroups of the Dene Athabascan people who traditionally lived in interior Alaska and parts of northern Canada and faced much harsher living conditions than those on the coast. They're known for following herds of caribou and moose for long distances through the Interior and Southcentral regions.

WITH OR WITHOUT THE APOSTROPHE

Mainland Yup'ik people prefer the spelling with the apostrophe. The Yupik people of St. Lawrence Island and the nearby coast of Chukotka in Russia prefer the spelling without the apostrophe.

ALASKA NATIVE VALUES

Here are just a few of the values that have been passed down from generation to generation that provide an excellent guide to live by.

- Be thankful
- Show respect for self, other people, animals, and the environment
- Be wise
- Be responsible for yourself and one another
- Be of good spirit
- Don't take more than you need
- Show humor

KEEPING NATIVE CULTURE ALIVE

There is a great effort to keep Native Alaskan culture alive and practice its traditions and values. Throughout Alaska, especially in rural villages, Alaska Natives hunt, fish and gather the same plants and animals their ancestors did. In some areas, subsistence hunting and gathering makes up more than 50 percent of Alaska Natives' diets.

. . .

Ceremonies and traditional gatherings remain a vibrant part of the culture. Elders pass on their knowledge of traditional art forms such as blanket weaving, beadwork, kayak-building, dancing, and wood and ivory carving.

MOST COMMON LAST NAMES

According to a 2019 report by the Alaska Department of Commerce, Community and Economic Development, the top three most common last names in Alaska in order are: Smith, Johnson, and Williams.

DID YOU KNOW?

Eskimo is a broad term used historically to refer to the Indigenous peoples who inhabit the circumpolar region of the Arctic, including Alaska, Canada, Greenland, and Siberia. But this term is increasingly considered outdated and potentially offensive, as it was imposed by outsiders and carries a derogatory connotation.

In neighboring Canada, the correct term for the Arctic people is Inuit. Most Alaskan Indigenous peoples prefer to be called by their specific names, such as Yupik, or collectively as Alaska Natives.

8

ALASKA HOLIDAYS & TRADITIONS

Official and Unofficial Alaskan Holidays

Like most US states, Alaska has a state holiday, but unlike other states, it has not just one, but two official state holidays: Seward's Day and Alaska Day.

SEWARD'S DAY

Seward's Day is marked on the last Monday of March. It celebrates the purchase of Alaska from Russia by the United States on March 30, negotiated by then–secretary of state William H. Seward.

Alaskans celebrate this day with parades, picnics, fish fries, fun runs, and other activities to embrace their state's history and heritage and have a good time with loved ones.

. . .

ALASKA DAY

Alaska Day is celebrated in Alaska on October 18. It commemorates the official transfer of Alaska from Russia to the United States on October 18, 1867. The holiday is celebrated with parades, speeches, and other events, and serves as a time for Alaskans to reflect on the state's history and heritage.

THE DAY THE RIVER OPENS

The Day the River Opens is an eagerly anticipated annual event in Alaska, marking the end of winter and the start of a new season filled with fishing, boating, and other outdoor activities. It is celebrated in a variety of ways that reflect the state's unique culture and love of the outdoors.

INDIGENOUS PEOPLE'S DAY

Alaska's Indigenous People's Day is a holiday that celebrates the rich history and culture of Native Alaskans. The holiday is observed on the second Monday in October, the same day as the federal Columbus Day holiday.

WINTER SOLSTICE

Winter solstice is the shortest day and longest night of the year, which falls on December 21 or 22. The way Alaskans celebrate it varies, depending on the culture and community. Some common traditions include potlatches, fire ceremonies, preparing traditional foods, and outdoor activities such as skiing, ice skating, and sledding. It's a time to celebrate the bounty of the harvest and the start of a new year, despite the long hours of darkness.

SUMMER SOLSTICE

Summer solstice is the longest day and shortest night of the year, falling on June 20 or 21. Alaskans celebrate by attending special events such as music festivals, street fairs, parades, and outdoor concerts; or participating in traditional ceremonies; outdoor activities like hiking, fishing, camping, and boating; having feasts and barbecues with friends and family; and celebrating art and culture. Parts of Alaska have up to 24 hours of daylight during this time.

FUR RONDY

The Fur Rendezvous Festival, or "Fur Rondy" for short, is an annual winter festival celebrated in Anchorage, usually in February. It is a celebration of the state's rich fur-trading history and features events such as dog sled races, ice sculptures, a parade, Indigenous cultural demonstrations, a fur auction, and winter sports.

The festival is a time for Alaskans to come together, celebrate their heritage, and enjoy the winter season. It's a fun-filled celebration that attracts locals and tourists alike and provides an opportunity to experience the unique culture and history of Alaska.

. . .

DIVIDEND DAY

Dividend Day is when residents receive an annual payment called the Permanent Fund Dividend, which comes from the state's oil wealth. This payment is managed by the Alaska Permanent Fund Corporation, and the day it is distributed varies each year but is typically in October.

The payment amount varies, but is usually between $1,000 and $2,000 per person, and all eligible residents who have lived in Alaska for at least one year receive it, regardless of income or job status.

Alaska's Traditions

FILL THE FREEZER

The "Fill the Freezer" tradition in Alaska is a way for residents to prepare for the long, harsh winter months ahead by stocking up on food. This typically involves hunting, fishing, and foraging for wild game and fish to preserve for the winter. The tradition is rooted in Alaska's history as a frontier state, where residents had to be self-sufficient and rely on their own resources to survive harsh conditions.

The Fill the Freezer tradition is often a communal activity, with friends and families gathering to help each other harvest and preserve food. The process can involve smoking, canning, or freezing food, and it is a time-honored way of preserving the state's natural bounty for future use.

. . .

NENANA ICE CLASSIC

The Nenana Ice Classic is a popular annual event in Nenana, Alaska, where people guess the time when the ice on the Tanana River will break up. The person who guesses the time most accurately wins a cash prize, which varies each year and can be over $300,000. The jackpot is funded by the sale of each ticket. As of 2023, the tickets were $3 each. The jackpot in 2023, was approximately $222,000.

To measure the exact time the ice breaks up, a tripod is planted in the ice in early March, when the ice is about two feet thick. The tripod is connected to a string that is connected to a clock. The clock is a standard wall clock that is encased in a protective box. When the ice breaks up, the tripod will move and the clock will stop. To ensure the ice has truly broken up, the clock doesn't stop until the tripod moves 100 feet or 30.48 meters downstream. The time on the clock will be the official time of the Tanana River ice breakup.

The event has been going on since 1917 and includes other fun activities such as live music and games. It's one of Alaska's longest running traditions and is a celebration of Alaska's culture and connection to nature.

BLANKET TOSS

The blanket toss is a traditional celebration game in Native Alaskan culture. It involves a large blanket held at its corners, used to toss people into the air. The goal is to see how high a person can be thrown and safely caught by the blanket bearers. It's a colorful and exciting spectacle that celebrates strength, skill, community, and the natural world. It's also a competitive event, where participants compete to be thrown the highest.

9

INDUSTRY AND ECONOMY

FISHING

If you love seafood, then Alaska is the place to be! There is more fish in those waters than you can shake a fishing rod at.

Fishing is one of Alaska's most important industries, and for good reason. Alaska's waters are some of the richest and most abundant in the world, with a variety of fish species that are highly sought after for their taste and nutritional value.

Alaska's fishing industry is primarily focused on wild-caught fish. People catch fish like salmon, halibut, pollock, cod, and crab to sell and eat. Fishing is important for the economy and for many Native Alaskans, who have been fishing these waters for many generations. Alaska has strict rules to protect fish stocks so fishing will remain sustainable. Alaska's fishing industry is known for having high-quality, sustainable seafood that is popular all over the world.

DID YOU KNOW?

There are over 30 different species of fish found in Alaskan waters.

OIL AND GAS

It may be freezing up in parts of Alaska, but they're sitting on a hot commodity! Alaska's oil and gas industry keeps us warm and cozy even in the coldest of winters. It is one of the state's most important economic drivers, generating billions of dollars in revenue each year.

The oil and gas industry in Alaska is primarily focused on the North Slope, a vast area of tundra and permafrost in the northern part of the state. The North Slope is home to several large oil and gas fields, including the Prudhoe Bay oil field, one of the largest oil fields in the world.

Companies extract oil and gas from the ground using drilling and pipelines. The industry creates jobs and supports other industries, but there are also environmental concerns about the impact on local ecosystems, the threat of major oil spills like the Exxon Valdez disaster in 1989, and the role of fossil fuels in climate change.

· · ·

TOURISM

Come for the scenery, stay for the moose! Alaska is a magnet for adventure-seekers and nature lovers alike.

Alaska's tourism industry attracts millions of visitors each year, who come to experience the state's stunning natural beauty and unique cultural heritage. Visitors can explore national parks, glaciers, and wildlife reserves, and learn about Alaska's history and traditions. The tourism industry supports businesses and jobs in Alaska, but visitors must also be careful to minimize their impact on the environment and respect the traditions of Native Alaskans.

DID YOU KNOW?
After the Caribbean, Alaska is the most popular cruise destination in the world.

MINING

They're not just panning for gold—Alaska is home to a variety of precious metals and minerals.

Alaska mines gold, silver, and platinum, as well as a variety of industrial minerals such as zinc, lead, and copper.

While mining in Alaska can be challenging due to the state's harsh climate and remote location, it provides jobs and economic benefits to local communities. However, there are concerns about its potential impact on the environment, so the state has implemented strict regulations to ensure that mining is done in a responsible and sustainable way.

ALASKA'S STATE GEM

Jade was designated as the state gemstone in 1968. Jade is a type of hard, usually green-colored mineral that has been valued for thousands of years by various cultures around the world, including the Indigenous peoples of Alaska.

Jade is found in several locations throughout Alaska. It is primarily used for jewelry and ornamental purposes, although in the past it was also used for tools and weapons.

Jade is sometimes referred to as the "stone of heaven" or the "emperor's stone," because it was believed to have mystical properties and was often used in religious and ceremonial contexts.

TIMBER

If you're a fan of lumberjacks and flannel shirts, you'll love Alaska's timber industry. They've got trees that go on for days (and days and days ...).

· · ·

Alaska's forests cover more than 100 million acres, making up about a third of the state's land area. These forests are predominantly softwood species such as spruce and hemlock, although there are also some hardwoods like birch and aspen.

To ensure the sustainability of the state's forests, the Alaska Division of Forestry manages timber harvests and enforces regulations to protect forest health and wildlife habitats. These efforts include replanting harvested areas, preserving sensitive areas, and monitoring forest health and wildlife populations.

DID YOU KNOW?

For those who want to learn more about the history of logging and see some of the world's best lumberjacks in action, Ketchikan has the Great Alaskan Lumberjack Show.

NO STATEWIDE SALES TAX

Alaska does not have a statewide sales tax, making it one of only five US states to not levy such a tax. This means that when you purchase goods or services in Alaska, you will not have to pay a sales tax on top of the advertised price.

Because Alaska gets a large amount of income from taxing natural resources, it doesn't need a statewide sales tax or state income tax. There are some local governments that do have their own sales tax, which can vary from 1 percent to as much as 7.5 percent. However, many rural areas of Alaska are completely free of sales tax.

NO STATE INCOME TAXES

Alaska is one of nine US states that doesn't have income taxes. This means residents get to keep a lot more of their paychecks.

PEONY FARMS

The newest blossoming industry seems to be in peonies. In 2000, there were zero peony farms, but this grew to more than 200 in 2014. Currently, there are more than 40 commercial peony farms across Alaska, and they grow around 1.5 million stems a year.

Peonies need cold weather to flourish, so during the busy wedding season between June and September, Alaska is the only place in the world to buy them.

DID YOU KNOW?

In many cultures, peonies are a symbol of love, prosperity, and good luck.

10

ALASKA & SPORTS

ALASKA'S OFFICIAL STATE SPORT: DOG MUSHING

Dogsledding is the official state sport in Alaska. Photo by Muro via depositphotos.com.

Dog mushing also known as dog sledding, is like a wintertime chariot race, but instead of horses, you have a pack of speedy sled dogs leading the way! It's the coolest sport in Alaska and the official state sport. Dog mushing is competitive, with many races held each year, including the famous Iditarod race that covers over 1,000 miles (1,609 km) of Alaskan wilderness.

PROFESSIONAL SPORT TEAMS

Currently, Alaska has no professional sports teams, however there are amateur and recreational sports leagues and events in various sports, including hockey, basketball, football, and baseball.

FISHING

Fishing is a big deal in Alaska, both as a sport and as an industry. Alaska has lots of fish species, like salmon and halibut, and people fish for fun, food, and money.

Many people come to Alaska expressly to go fishing, and there are many places to fish, from freshwater streams to saltwater bays. There are also plenty of businesses that offer fishing trips and experiences.

HOCKEY

Alaska is home to numerous hockey leagues and teams, including the Alaska Aces, a former professional team.

. . .

CROSS-COUNTRY SKIING

With its abundance of snow and scenic terrain, cross-country skiing is a popular winter sport in Alaska.

SNOWBOARDING AND SKIING

With numerous ski resorts and backcountry skiing opportunities, Alaska offers excellent opportunities for snowboarding and skiing enthusiasts.

HUNTING

Hunting has been a part of Alaska's history for a long time, and many Alaskans rely on it for food and other resources. Out of respect for the animal, there is a code rooted in Indigenous values that says you only hunt what you need and use every part of the animal.

Alaska has a diverse range of game animals, and commercial hunting is an important industry. The state has strict wildlife management policies to ensure sustainable hunting and protect wildlife populations. Hunting licenses and tags generate revenue for the state, and many Alaskan communities benefit economically from hunting-related activities.

RUNNING AND CYCLING

Alaska's scenic trails, roads, and landscapes make it an ideal destination for runners, cyclists, and other outdoor enthusiasts.

· · ·

SNOWMOBILE RACING

Snowmobile racing—or snowmachine racing, as it is known in
Alaska—is a popular winter sport where drivers race in various
styles, such as cross-country, sprint, and hill-climbing. The
races can be short or long, covering hundreds of miles over
several days. Many Alaskans enjoy watching the races, which
usually take place on weekends and are accompanied by other
fun winter activities like snowmachine demonstrations, live
music, and tasty food. Both amateur and professional riders
compete for prizes and glory.

THE IRON DOG SNOWMOBILE RACE

Iron Dog takes place in Alaska every year, covering a 2,000-
mile (3,218 km) course from Big Lake to Nome. It is considered
the toughest snowmobile race in the world, attracting riders
from all over the world.

The race takes place in February and requires riders to navigate
through challenging terrain, such as snow-covered forests,
frozen rivers, and treacherous mountain passes. Iron Dog is a
team event with two riders on each snowmobile, and the
winners receive several thousand dollars in prize money.

The race is highly competitive, and winning it is a major
accomplishment for any snowmobile racer. Riders participate
for the thrill of competition, the love of snowmobiling, and the
chance to showcase their skills.

. . .

BASKETBALL AND FOOTBALL

Basketball and football are popular team sports in Alaska, with local leagues, high school and college teams, and recreational leagues.

DID YOU KNOW?

School and community sports teams have to fly or take the ferry to compete with other teams from other towns.

SKIJORING

Skijoring in Alaska. Photo by travelarium via depositphotos.com.

Alaska Skijoring is a winter sport that combines cross-country skiing and horseback riding or dog sledding. Participants wear skis and hold onto a rope that is attached to a horse or dog (or even another animal). The horse or dog pulls the skier across the snow at high speeds, and together they navigate through a course filled with jumps and other obstacles. The sport originated in Norway and was brought to Alaska in the early 1900s. Today, it is a popular winter recreational activity, and there are various skijoring competitions held throughout Alaska and other northern regions.

ICE GOLF

Alaska Ice Golf is a winter sport played on frozen lakes and ponds. It is similar to traditional golf, but played on ice, with modified equipment such as plastic balls, short clubs, and holes drilled into the ice. Participants tee off and aim to get their ball into the ice holes in as few strokes as possible. The sport is typically played outdoors in sub-zero temperatures and has become a popular pastime in Alaska and other northern regions during the long, dark, winter months.

THE BERING SEA ICE CLASSIC GOLF TOURNAMENT

The Bering Sea Ice Classic is an annual ice golf event held in Nome during Iditarod Week. It's an Alaskan twist on the traditional game, where golfers play on the ice of the frozen Bering Sea. The tournament typically attracts golfers from all over Alaska and beyond, and is held in March when the ice on the sea is at its thickest—at least three feet.

. . .

It's a unique and challenging event, as the ice can be uneven and conditions on the Bering Sea can be harsh, with wind, snow, and low temperatures. Despite the challenges, the Bering Sea Ice Classic is a fun and lighthearted event that celebrates the rugged beauty of the Alaskan winter and the spirit of adventure of its residents.

The game consists of six holes and is played with bright green balls, but the challenge is finding them, as they tend to roll into cracks or get lost in snow drifts. The "green" in the Bering Sea Ice Classic is a small piece of green carpet laid out over the uneven ice near each hole. Shotgun shells and miniature liquor bottles are used as tees, while coffee cans frozen into the ice serve as holes, with no hole being farther than 120 yards (110 m) apart. One of the holes is often placed in the "Nome National Forest," a group of last year's Christmas trees hammered into the ice after the holidays.

The rules of the game are unique, such as a three-stroke penalty for hitting a polar bear. Also, players are required to take a mandatory break at a local bar between holes to warm their fingers and toes. The Bering Sea Ice Classic has been a staple during Iditarod Week for over 30 years, and it's all about having fun rather than intense competition.

WORLD ESKIMO-INDIAN OLYMPICS

The World Eskimo-Indian Olympics (WEIO), alternatively named the World Exhibition of Indigenous Olympics, is an annual athletic event in Alaska that celebrates the traditional games, dance, and culture of the Indigenous peoples of the Arctic region.

The event brings together top Indigenous athletes from Alaska, Northern Canada, Greenland, and Siberia to participate in a series of competitions that test their strength, endurance, balance, and pain tolerance. The games take place at the Big Dipper Ice Arena in Fairbanks every summer in mid-July.

The event features a wide range of athletic competitions, including traditional games like the One-Foot High Kick, the Alaskan High Kick, the Two-Foot High Kick, the Arctic Shot Put, the Four Man Carry, the Eskimo Stick Pull, and more.

The event also showcases traditional dance, music, storytelling, and craft demonstrations. The WEIO has been held for over 50 years and is an important gathering for Indigenous peoples to share their culture, traditions, and heritage with each other and with the world.

THE FOUR MAN CARRY

One of the most exciting events is the Four Man Carry, where a single athlete is tasked with carrying four people at once for as long as possible, simulating the weight of carrying meat back to camp after a successful hunting expedition.

. . .

ESKIMO STICK PULL

Another popular competition is the Eskimo Stick Pull, which challenges athletes to demonstrate their strength and endurance by trying to pull a stick away from their opponent, similar to the difficulty of pulling a seal out of the water.

11

ALASKA'S FAMOUS IDITAROD SLED DOG RACE

FAMOUS SLED DOG RACE

The Iditarod Trail Sled Dog Race is like the Olympics of dog sledding, happening every March in Alaska. It's not your average race, either, covering more than 1,000 miles of snowy terrain from Anchorage to Nome.

If you want to compete, you'd better be ready for a wild ride, because this is one of the toughest sled dog races in the world! The mushers and their trusty dogs must be in top shape both physically and mentally to make it to the finish line. And, speaking of finish line, the first team to make it to Nome gets all the glory and prizes.

But the Iditarod is more than just a race; it's also a tribute to Alaska's heritage and the vital role sled dogs have played in its history.

. . .

IDITAROD MEANS 'DISTANT PLACE'

Iditarod is a city, a river, a trail and a race all in the same area.
Iditarod is derived from the Athabaskan language and is
believed to mean "far-off place" or "distant place." The name
refers to the Iditarod River and the historic Iditarod Trail,
which were used to transport goods and people between coastal
towns and interior settlements in Alaska during the gold
rush era.

THE MUSHERS AND THEIR TEAM OF DOGS

Each musher starts with a team of 12 to 14 dogs, but can drop
dogs that are tired or injured along the way. They cannot add
new dogs during the race. At least five dogs must be in the team
at the finish line.

HOW MANY COMPETE

Around 50 to 60 teams of mushers and dogs usually start the
Iditarod Trail Sled Dog Race each year. The teams usually
average 14 dogs each, which means over 1,000 dogs start the
race.

Due to the challenging conditions, not all teams are able to
finish the race. Typically, around 30 to 40 teams complete the
race each year.

. . .

THE MUSHERS

To qualify to race in the Iditarod, a musher must be at least 18 years old and must complete three qualifying races. Most mushers are from Alaska, but mushers from around the world have come to compete in the Iditarod.

DID YOU KNOW?

The Iditarod is one of only a handful of major sporting events where men and women compete side by side.

THE DOGS OF THE IDITAROD

While most people assume Siberian huskies are the most common breed of dog to run the Iditarod, it's the Alaskan husky that is the most common. While not recognized as an official breed by the American Kennel Club, it's the most common sled dog used in the Iditarod and other modern sled dog races. You will still find a few Siberian huskies used, but they are not the norm.

ONLY DOGS SUITABLE FOR ARCTIC TRAVEL

After musher John Suter used European poodles on his dogsled team in 1988 and had to drop off several of them at checkpoints due to frozen feet and hair-matting problems, the rules were changed so that not just any type of dog could be used.

· · ·

The Iditarod isn't any old sled dog race, and it's important the right dogs are used, for their safety and for the safety of the mushers.

According to the 2023 Iditarod Rules, only dogs suited to arctic travel are permitted to enter the race, and suitability is determined by race officials.

HAW AND GEE

When mushing, the command "Haw" signals the dogs to turn left. "Gee" is what's said to turn right. Often you hear them as "Haw, haw" or "Gee, gee!"

DID YOU KNOW?
Sled dogs who are unable to continue racing are dropped off at the closest checkpoints to be cared for. If they are near Eagle River, the dogs are sent to the Hiland Mountain Correctional Center and cared for by female inmates until they can be picked up later by their handlers.

WHAT DO THEY TAKE?

Iditarod mushers can carry differing amounts of weight on their sleds, depending on their plans, the dogs they have, and trail conditions. But they must carry specific required gear, including a warm sleeping bag, an ax, snow shoes, dog booties, insulated dog coats, and other safety equipment, which can weigh up to 20 pounds (9 kg).

On top of that, mushers must carry enough food and supplies for themselves and their dogs for eight to 14 days, which can weigh several hundred pounds. But they can leave some supplies at checkpoints to make the load lighter. The overall weight carried by mushers can range from around 30 to 100 pounds (13 to 45 kg) or more, depending on many factors.

INSULATED DOG COAT

An insulated dog coat for each dog on the team is now part of the mandatory items that each musher must have with them during the race.

DOG BOOTIES

Iditarod dogs wear colorful booties while racing to protect their feet from the snow and ice that can damage their paw pads or get between their toes. The rules state that the musher must have at least eight pairs of booties for each dog at all times, in the sled or in use, though often the dogs will go through a lot more than this over the course of the race.

SPECIAL DOG FOOD FOR THE TRAIL

Iditarod sled dogs burn roughly 12,000 calories during the race and need to be fed well with snacks throughout the day. It's impossible to carry all the food needed for the entire race, so mushers have bags of dog food shipped to checkpoints along the trail. The dogs are fed a high-protein diet that may include red meat, fish, beaver, and sometimes seal blubber, mixed with regular dog food and water. The food is heated and often looks like a mush. The liquid mixed with the food keeps the dogs hydrated, as they rarely drink plain water in winter.

THE RACE ROUTES

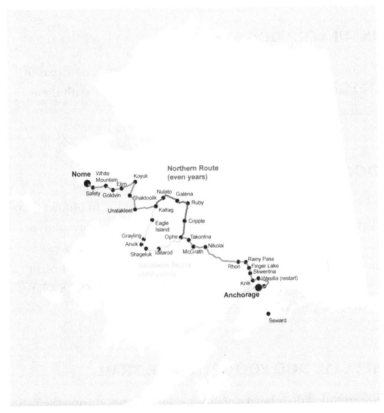

Iditarod sled dog race route throughout Alaska.

There is a northern route and a southern route, and the race alternates between the two routes depending on the year. On even-numbered years, racers use the northern route. The southern route is used on odd-numbered years. Both follow the same trail for the first 352 miles (566 km) from Anchorage to Ophir, and then they split. The routes meet again at Kaltag, which is 346 miles (557 km) from Nome. So both routes start in Anchorage and end in Nome.

TWO MOUNTAIN RANGES

Not only does the race run along the Yukon River and over the frozen Norton Sound, it crosses two mountain ranges, including the Alaska Range, which happens to be North America's largest mountain range.

1,049 SYMBOLIC DISTANCE

The Iditarod has a symbolic distance of 1,049 miles. The 1,000 miles signifies that the race is roughly 1,000 miles, and the 49 commemorates Alaska as the 49th US. state. The actual distance varies depending on the year and which route is being followed.

CHECKPOINTS

There are checkpoints along the trail that all teams must pass through, signing in as they go. This gives the mushers and their dogs a chance to camp, eat, and rest. It's also where race officials can keep track of the teams, their progress, and how the dogs are doing. There are 26 checkpoints on the northern route and 27 on the southern route.

MANDATORY BREAKS

During the Iditarod, teams must make three rest stops. The first stop is a mandatory 24-hour break that can be taken at any checkpoint. The second stop is an eight-hour break that must be taken at a checkpoint on the Yukon River. The third stop is another eight-hour break that is required at White Mountain, the final stop before the finish line in Nome.

Throughout the rest of the race, mushers and their dogs have very little opportunity to rest, and often do not sleep at all. They may take short breaks at checkpoints to eat meals, but otherwise, the race requires them to keep moving forward through the rugged and challenging terrain.

CEREMONIAL START

Every year, on the first Saturday in March, the Iditarod race starts in downtown Anchorage at 10 a.m. Alaska Standard time. This is the only part of the race that takes place in a city setting, and it is a chance for spectators to watch the teams go by. The first to depart is an honorary musher, followed by the competitors, who leave at a rate of one team every two minutes.

The teams take it easy during this 11-mile (17.7 km) stretch, and it does not count towards the official race time. The starting positions are determined by a drawing, and an IditaRider rides with the mushers in the front of their sled during the ceremonial start.

IDITARIDER

One way to support the Last Great Race and enjoy the best view of the Iditarod is being the highest bidder in the Idita-Rider auction. Winning bidders secure the best "seat in the house" and get to ride in the sled of an Iditarod musher for the first 11 miles (17.7 km) of the race through Anchorage.

Using the 2023 Iditarod as an example, winning bids have ranged from a few thousand dollars to over seven thousand dollars to ride with 2022's Iditarod winner, Brent Sass, who competed again in 2023.

SNOW IS TRUCKED IN

To ensure there is enough snow for the teams to run on through Anchorage's city streets, snow is trucked in the night before and spread along the road for the mushers.

RESTART

The restart is the official start of the Iditarod race and takes place in Willow, Alaska, which is about 50 miles (80 km) north of Anchorage. This is where the mushers and their teams begin their 1,000-mile (1,609 km) journey through the Alaskan wilderness, racing to the finish line in Nome. The restart is where the race clock starts ticking, and it is from this point that the mushers begin their timed race to the finish.

THE FINISH

The official Iditarod finish line is the Red "Fox" Olson Trail Monument, aka the "Burled Arch" in Nome, Alaska. The arch has the words "End of Iditarod Sled Dog Race" etched onto it.

Burled Arch in Nome, Alaska. Photo by Chris Fuller via influenceleadership.com

THE WIDOW'S LAMP

The "Widow's Lamp" is lit and hangs on the arch until the last competitor crosses the finish line. The lamp is lit in Nome at 10 a.m. on the Saturday the race begins and attached to the Burled Arch. It remains lit as long as there are mushers on the trail.

THE RED LANTERN

According to tradition, the last musher to cross the finish line receives the "Committed Through the Last Mile" Red Lantern Award and also given the honor of extinguishing the widow's lamp. What started as a joke has become to symbolize perseverance—the joke being that the last-place finisher was so far behind that they needed to light his way home.

THE PRIZES

The musher who comes in first place typically wins a cash prize and as of 2016, a new truck. The exact amount of the cash prize can vary from year to year, depending on the total purse available for the race, which is divided among the top finishers.

In recent years, the winner's cash prize has ranged from around $50,000 to over $70,000. It's customary that the last place finishers, are awarded the symbolic $1,049. (The Iditarod has a symbolic distance of 1,049 miles.) In 2023, the total prize purse came to $500,000 and was split between 29 finishers. The first-place winner, was awarded $51,800.

The lead dog or dogs of the winning team are awarded the "Golden Harness" as well as a celebratory cupcake in the shape of an Alaskan Malamute.

AWARDS OF GOLD NUGGETS, SALMON, & CASH

The Iditarod race is sponsored by a variety of companies and there are several different awards given throughout the race with different types of prizes for each.

For example, Ryan Redington, the 2023 Iditarod winner, not only crossed the finish line first, but along the route, he won the Alaska Air Transit Spirit of Iditarod Award, Bristol Bay Native Corporation Fish First Award, Ryan Air Gold Coast Award and the Northrim Bank Achieve More Award. His winnings from those awards totaled $5,000 in cash, $1,000 in gold nuggets and 25 pounds of salmon.

THE VERY FIRST RACE

The first Iditarod race began on March 3, 1973, with 34 teams; 22 teams finished 32 days later.

THE SLOWEST WINNING TIME

The slowest winning time of 20 days, 15 hours, two minutes and seven seconds was recorded in 1974 by Carl Huntington.

THE FASTEST WINNING TIME

The fastest winning time was recorded in 2017 by Mitch Seavey, with eight days, three hours, 40 minutes and 13 seconds, breaking the previous record, set by Dallas Seavey, of eight days, 11 hours, 20 minutes and 16 seconds.

. . .

THE YOUNGEST MUSHER

The youngest musher to ever compete in the Iditarod was Dallas Seavey, in 2005, when he turned 18 the day before the race began on March 5, 2005. He was also the youngest winner, in 2012, at the age of 25.

THE OLDEST MUSHER

The oldest musher to ever compete is Colonel Norman D. Vaughan, who last competed in 1992 at the age of 86.

IDITAROD AIR FORCE

The Iditarod Air Force is a group of volunteer pilots and planes that help the Iditarod race by delivering important supplies and medical help to remote checkpoints along the trail. They fly in tough and isolated conditions, and are crucial for the safety and success of the mushers and dogs.

MOTHER OF THE IDITAROD – DOROTHY G. PAGE

Dorothy wanted to celebrate the 100th anniversary of the purchase of Alaska from Russia with a spectacular dog race, to recognize what mushers and their dogs had done for Alaska.

She founded the Iditarod Trail Committee in 1967, and with the help of other mushers, the first Iditarod race took place in 1973.

· · ·

Today, the Iditarod is one of the most famous and toughest sled dog races in the world. Dorothy was an Alaskan musher and breeder of sled dogs and is known as the "Mother of the Iditarod," even though she never competed in the race herself.

LIBBY RIDDLES – THE FIRST WOMAN TO WIN THE IDITAROD

March 20, 1985, is when Libby Riddles crossed the finish line with her dog team and became the first woman to win the Iditarod. Her win came in part because she was the only musher who chose to continue during a bad blizzard.

JR. IDITAROD

For those who are passionate about dog sledding but haven't reached the minimum age of 18 to race in the Iditarod, the Jr. Iditarod is open to youth 14 years and older.

The race is about 160 miles long and welcomes young mushers from around the world. Several junior mushers have gone on to race in the Iditarod, including a few famous winners such as Dallas Seavey and Lance Mackey.

No monetary prizes are awarded to the Jr. Iditarod winner, but scholarships are awarded to the top five finishers.

· · ·

NOT EVERYONE FINISHES THE RACE ALIVE

Since its inception in 1973, more than 150 sled dogs have died in the Iditarod race. The causes of death include fatigue, exposure, hypothermia, and other health issues related to the harsh Alaskan wilderness. As of 2023, no humans have died in the Iditarod race.

12

FAMOUS INVENTIONS MADE IN ALASKA

ULU KNIFE

Traditional Alaskan Ulu knife

A traditional Alaska Native knife used for a variety of tasks, including skinning animals and cutting food.

. . .

XTRATUF BOOTS

Xtratuf boots on a tour boat at the north end of Glacier Bay. Photo by John Kupersmith via Flickr.

Invented by clothing company XTRATUF in the mid-1900s, XTRATUF rubber boots and clothing were designed to protect fishermen and other outdoor workers from the harsh Alaskan weather.

IGLOO

The igloo, a dome-shaped shelter made of snow blocks, is traditionally associated with the Inuit and other Indigenous peoples of the Arctic, including those in Alaska, who used it for thousands of years as temporary shelter for hunting and other activities. They continue to be used in some parts of the world today.

. . .

While the igloo is not a modern invention or technology, it is an
important part of the cultural and historical heritage of Alaska
and other Arctic regions.

SNOW GOGGLES

Invented by Inuit hunters in the pre-colonial era, snow goggles
are a type of eye protection designed to prevent snow blindness
and eye damage caused by the glare of the sun on the snow.

PARKA

Invented by Indigenous people in the Arctic and sub-Arctic
regions, the parka is a type of warm and waterproof jacket
designed to protect people from the cold and wet conditions of
the northern wilderness. It is traditionally made of caribou or
seal skin; the word parka is derived from an Aleut language,
meaning "animal skin." The coat goes by different names across
the Far North.

MUSKOX YARN

Made from the soft underwool of the muskox, a large Arctic
mammal, muskox yarn is used for making warm clothing and
other items. It was first commercially produced in Alaska in the
late 1960s and has since become a popular choice for those
looking for warm, natural-fiber products.

13

TRAINS, PLANES AND SNOWMACHINES

Alaskans live in a rugged and wild place and so sometimes have to get creative with their modes of transportation. There are a variety of ways to get around, including float plane, boat, snowmachine, dog sled, and moose-buggy.

DOG SLED

Dog mushing has been a mode of transportation in Alaska for centuries, especially during the harsh winter months. It was originally used by Indigenous people to travel and hunt, and later became a crucial means of transportation during the gold rush. Sled dogs were used to transport goods and supplies to remote areas that were inaccessible by other means. They also played a vital role in delivering mail and supplies to isolated communities, and in rescue missions during emergencies.

· · ·

Today, dog mushing continues to be a significant part of
Alaska's history and culture, and is still used as a mode of transportation in remote areas where roads and other forms of transportation are limited.

SNOWMACHINES

Snowmachines, also known as snowmobiles or sleds, are a
popular mode of transportation in rural and remote areas of
Alaska, particularly in the winter months, when snow and ice
make road travel difficult. Many Alaskans own snowmachines
and use them for transportation, recreation, and work. Snowmachines are also used by hunters, fishermen, and other
outdoor enthusiasts to access remote areas.

LICENSE TO DRIVE SNOWMACHINES?

In Alaska, you don't need a special snowmachine license to
drive a snowmachine, but you do need a valid driver's license if
you're 16 or older. If you're under 16, you need to take a safety
course and carry a safety certificate while driving.

Even though a special snowmachine license isn't required,
snowmobile drivers must follow traffic laws and safety rules,
just like other vehicles. This includes having insurance, regis-
tration, and operating responsibly.

It's also illegal to drive a snowmobile while under the influence
of drugs or alcohol.

. . .

MOOSE-BUGGY

Moose-buggies are basically modified off-road 4x4 vehicles that are made to access very remote and difficult areas such as thick Alaska forests or boggy swamps. These vehicles also need to be able to haul a 900-pound (408 kg) moose out. As a reminder, these animals can weigh anywhere between 800 and 1,100 pounds (363 and 500 kg).

AI rendition of a moose-buggy

Moose-buggies have giant tires, a roll bar or cage, a crane and a winch. These giant tires can sometimes be 50 inches (127 cm) to keep them from getting stuck in mud bogs. The roll cage is to protect passengers in case the vehicle rolls and you end up upside-down. The crane-and-winch system is what you can use to haul your trophy moose out of the woods and back home to fill yours and your neighbors' freezers.

. . .

SO MANY PILOTS

People in Alaska often have to fly to get to their destination. Normally, it's only by plane that mail and other things can be delivered. For this reason, there are many pilots in Alaska. As of December 2021, there were 9,153 certified pilots, out of a population of 733,673. This means that one in every 80 people in Alaska is a certified pilot. That's six times as many pilots per capita as anywhere else in the US.

WHERE THERE ARE PILOTS, THERE ARE AIRPORTS

Almost every town in Alaska has an airport, which means that Alaska has the most airports in the US per capita. There are over 400 airports in Alaska. These include:

- 4 international airports
- 237 public airports
- 57 heliports
- 132 seaplane bases

ALASKA AIRLINES' MILK RUN

The Alaska Airlines' Milk Run is a series of daily supply flights that connect Seattle, Anchorage, and several smaller towns in Southeast Alaska. The Alaska Milk Run is not just one route, but six individual Milk Run routes that serve different destinations between Seattle and Anchorage. These routes include stops at small island communities including Ketchikan, Sitka, Wrangell, Petersburg, Yakutat, and Juneau.

. . .

The Milk Run is named after a term in the airline industry that refers to a regularly scheduled flight with many stops. Though the name suggests that the Milk Run carries milk, it actually carries a variety of essential goods and supplies, such as food, medicine, and building supplies.

DID YOU KNOW?

One leg of the Milk Run route is only 11 minutes in duration. The 11-minute flight between Ketchikan and Wrangell is only about 50 miles, and the flight takes advantage of the prevailing winds to make the trip super quick.

STEEP CLIMBS AND SHORT RUNWAYS

The Alaska Milk Run also happens to include some of the steepest takeoffs and shortest runways in the United States. As an example, the airport in Yakutat is located in a valley, and the surrounding mountains rise up to 10,000 feet. This means that planes have to climb very steeply in order to clear the mountains and reach cruising altitude.

The shortest runway on the Milk Run is the Petersburg Airport. The standard length for a commercial runway is 5,000 feet. The runway at Petersburg Airport is only 3,600 feet long

. . .

BUSH PILOTS

Bush pilots fly smaller aircraft into rugged and harsh terrain, often referred to as the "bush." Bush pilots are a lifeline to rural villages and are how people, essential supplies and food are delivered to hard-to-reach places in Alaska. Bush pilots operate rescue missions, are part of the tourism industry, fly kids to school, get pregnant woman safely to hospitals and so much more.

BUSH PLANES

Float plane on a lake. Photo by Jake Buonemani on Unsplash.

Bush planes have to be able to take off and land in short places. Bush planes are often fitted with tundra tires, floats or skies to make it possible to land on dry, rough ground, snow, and ice.

. . .

WORLD'S LARGEST SEAPLANE BASE

Lake Hood in Anchorage is not only the world's largest seaplane base, but also the busiest. On average, there are 190 flights per day. During winter, when the lake is frozen, airplanes with skis are still able to land and use the base.

ICE ROADS

Ice roads are temporary roads in Alaska used during winter months. They are used to access remote locations or areas inaccessible by regular roads. Ice roads are usually built over rivers, lakes, or other bodies of water and are maintained by clearing snow, monitoring the thickness and stability of the ice, and monitoring traffic.

COMMUNITY ICE ROADS

There are the big ice roads seen on TV, and then there are the community ice roads that are for the people. One example is the frozen surface of the Kuskokwim River, which is groomed each year and made into the temporary Kuskokwim ice road, which serves over 17 villages and can stretch as long as 300 miles (482 km).

This road is for the communities that live nearby and makes life much more convenient and cheaper. Not just ice trucks use this road, but snowmachines and other vehicles, using it to carry mail, get to a hospital or clinic, and even to transport school teams to basketball games in nearby villages. There is no other road connecting the communities.

. . .

ICE ROAD TRUCKERS

Ice road drivers work between mid-January and mid-March, when it's safe to drive on the ice. The season is short, but the pay can range from $20,000 to $80,000.

Ice road drivers haul 1.8 million pound (816,466 kg) loads, facing numerous dangers including whiteouts, avalanches and frigid temperatures (think -100°F, or -73°C with wind chill) that can cause major and sometimes fatal issues.

TRAINS

The Alaska Railroad provides both passenger and freight services in Alaska, with routes connecting major cities such as Anchorage, Fairbanks, and Seward.

The railroad offers scenic train tours and wilderness excursions, providing travelers with breathtaking views of Alaska's rugged landscape and wildlife.

However, the train services in Alaska are limited compared to other regions, as much of the state is wild and remote, and accessible only by plane or boat. The Alaska Railroad is an important mode of transportation for goods and supplies, as well as a popular tourist attraction, offering visitors a unique and unforgettable way to experience Alaska.

. . .

GOLD RUSH BICYCLING

During the Klondike Gold Rush in the late 1890s, many prospectors traveled through Alaska to Canada's Yukon Territory in search of gold. One of these prospectors, W. J. Terry, rode his bicycle from Skagway, Alaska, to Dawson City, Yukon, a distance of over 300 miles (483 km).

This journey was a remarkable feat, as the terrain was rugged and often impassable. Terry's gold rush journey helped demonstrate the versatility and durability of the bicycle as a means of transportation. His journey was widely reported in the press and inspired others to use bicycles for transportation in Alaska and beyond.

DID YOU KNOW?

The US mail gets delivered a variety of ways in Alaska: by road, air, boat, dog sled and snowmachine. In the past, the mail has even been delivered by a sled pulled by reindeer.

14

RANDOM AND AWESOME

BOB ROSS AND HIS ALASKAN "HAPPY LITTLE TREES"

Bob Ross was born in Florida and died in Florida, but his time spent in Alaska during his military career changed his life. It was in Alaska when he first saw the snow and mountains that often appeared in his paintings. He attended an art class in Anchorage and developed an interest in painting. He began painting and soon started successfully selling Alaskan landscapes painted on touristy gold-mining pans.

The income from his painting eventually surpassed his military salary, so he retired from the military, moved back to Florida, studied painting seriously and began to paint full time.

ALASKA'S MOST POPULAR DOG BREEDS

According to the American Kennel Club, these are the top

three most popular dogs among Alaskans: Labradors, ranking number one; followed by German shepherds, then golden retrievers.

SLED-DOG BREEDS

Some of the best-known sled-dog breeds include the Samoyed, Alaskan malamute, Siberian husky, Alaskan husky and Chinook. These dogs have what it takes to run hundreds of miles across packed ice and frozen terrain in arctic temperatures.

MORE CARIBOU THAN PEOPLE

According to the Alaska Department of Fish and Game, the caribou population in Alaska is estimated to be around 950,000, while the human population in Alaska is estimated to be around 730,000.

ALASKA'S CAT MAYOR

The town of Talkeetna elected a cat named Stubbs as their honorary mayor. Stubbs was elected by residents in 1997 as a write-in candidate, in an expression of dissatisfaction with the human candidates running for office.

Stubbs served as honorary mayor of Talkeetna for 20 years, until his passing in 2017 at the age of 20. During his time in office, Stubbs became a beloved local celebrity and helped to bring attention and tourism to the small town.

. . .

Although Stubbs was not an official mayor with any political power, he was a symbol of the town's unique spirit and independent character.

A TOWN CALLED CHICKEN

Chicken-Alaska by Arthur D. Chapman and Audrey Bendus via Flickr (CC by 2.0)

Chicken is a small community in the eastern part of the state, near the Canadian border. The town was founded in the late 1800's during the gold rush. The plan was to name it after the state bird, the ptarmigan, but the miners struggled with the spelling. So they decided to call the town "chicken" because they all knew how to spell that. Today, Chicken is a popular tourist destination.

. . .

THE ONLY STATE THAT CAN BE TYPED OUT USING ONLY ONE ROW OF KEYS

If you use a QWERTY keyboard, which most of us do, you may be surprised to learn that Alaska can be typed out ONLY using letters from the middle line. No other U.S. state can say the same.

RECORD-BREAKING VEGETABLES GROWN IN ALASKA

Giant pumpkins on top of wood pallets

Alaska's Matanuska Valley is famous for its giant vegetables, such as cabbages, pumpkins, carrots, turnips, and beets, which grow enormous thanks to the area's long summer days, rich soil, and cool climate.

. . .

Some of the vegetables have broken world records, with some cabbages weighing over 100 pounds (45 kg) and some pumpkins weighing over 2,000 pounds (907 kg).

To check out Alaska's record-breaking vegetables in person, it's worth visiting Alaska's State Fair in Palmer, Alaska in late August/early September.

The giant vegetables have become a popular tourist attraction and symbolize Alaska's unique agriculture and ability to grow crops in challenging conditions.

15

YOU KNOW YOU'RE IN ALASKA WHEN...

LOCALS ALWAYS PUT THEIR TRASH IN BEAR-PROOF CONTAINERS

In Alaska, bears are common in many areas, and they have a strong sense of smell that attracts them to food sources.

To prevent bears from accessing trash, Alaskans use bear-proof containers that are designed to be secure and resist being opened by bears. These containers are made of heavy-duty materials, such as steel or heavy-duty plastic, and have locking lids or other secure features that prevent bears from accessing the contents.

LOCALS PLUG IN THEIR VEHICLES AT NIGHT

Plugging in vehicles during winter is a common practice to prevent the engine and other components from freezing. Winter temperatures in Alaska can drop to extremely low levels, causing engine oil, transmission fluid, and other fluids to freeze. This can cause significant damage to the engine and other systems, rendering the vehicle inoperable.

No, these aren't electric cars. Cars need to be plugged during conditions of extreme cold to keep the engines from freezing. Photo by Robert Drozda via Flickr.

By plugging in an engine block heater and battery maintainer, the engine and other components stay warm enough to prevent freezing and allow the vehicle to start more easily.

YOU CAN RUN WITH REINDEER

Reindeer running is a unique activity in Alaska, where participants run or jog alongside domesticated reindeer. This activity is often held as part of events or tours that take place in areas with large populations of reindeer, such as the Alaskan tundra. The reindeer used in these events are trained and used to being around people, making it a fun and safe experience.

Running of the Reindeer 2013, Anchorage, Alaska. Photo by Sgt. 1st Class Jason Epperson via Flickr (CC by 2.0)

PLANES HAVE SKIS

Many small towns and villages in Alaska are inaccessible by road, so planes are an important mode of transportation.

Bush plane in Alaska landing on a field of snow using skis. Photo via
DepositPhotos.com

In the winter, when the ground is covered in snow and ice, skis
are attached to the bottom of planes to allow them to land on
snow-covered runways and other snowy surfaces. This is
known as a ski-plane or a bush plane, and it is a common sight
in Alaska, especially in more remote areas of the state. Ski-
equipped planes are also used for hunting, fishing, and other
outdoor activities in Alaska's vast wilderness.

HANG SALMON OUTSIDE TO DRY

In Alaska, many people engage in traditional subsistence
fishing and hunting practices, including fishing for salmon.
One traditional method of preserving salmon is to hang it to
dry. This process involves gutting the salmon, cutting it into
strips, and hanging the strips in the sun and wind to dry. The
process concentrates the flavor of the salmon and makes it
easier to store for later use. Dried salmon can be eaten as a
snack or used in traditional dishes such as soups and stews.

. . .

BUNNY BOOTS AND XTRATUF ARE YOUR TWO FAVORITE BOOTS

"Bunny boots" and "Xtratuf" are types of boots commonly worn in Alaska. "Bunny boots" are thick, insulated rubber boots designed to keep your feet warm in extremely cold temperatures.

White "Bunny Boots" via Wikimedia Commons

"Xtratuf" boots are waterproof boots often worn by fishermen and other outdoor workers. Xtratuf boots are also sometimes jokingly referred to as "Alaskan sneakers."

Classic Xtratuf waterproof boots. Photo by Ritch via Flickr.

16

FUN FOOD AND DRINK FACTS

BIRCH SYRUP

Wild-harvest birch syrup made from the sap of Alaska's birch trees is a pure and sweet treat.

SPRUCE TIP JELLY

Just like it sounds, spruce tip jelly is a type of jelly made from the tips of spruce trees. The tips are harvested in the spring, when they are still light green and tender and have a citrusy, resinous flavor. The flavor of the jelly can vary depending on the type of spruce used, but it is often described as tart, sweet, and slightly floral.

FIREWEED

Many cultures connect this abundant and resilient plant, one of the first to spring up after a devastating fire, to the idea of life after death. Fireweed is often made into jelly, honey, or syrups, and used in ice cream and milkshakes.

FIREWEED HONEY

Fireweed honey is a type of honey unique to Alaska. It is made from the nectar of the fireweed flower, which grows abundantly in Alaska during the summer.

FIREWEED JELLY

Made from the nectar of the fireweed flower, this jelly has a sweet and floral flavor.

CLOUDBERRY JAM

Cloudberry is a fruit that grows in the tundra regions of Alaska. The jam has a tart, sweet, and slightly floral flavor.

SALMONBERRY JAM

Salmonberry is a native fruit in Alaska, and its jam has a tart and sweet taste.

LOWBUSH CRANBERRY JAM

Also known as lingonberry, this jam is tangy and tart, similar to cranberry sauce.

· · ·

WILD BLUEBERRY JAM

Alaska has wild blueberries that are smaller and more flavorful than cultivated blueberries. Their jam has a strong, sweet flavor.

PILOT BREAD

Pilot bread is a type of hardtack that is a staple food in Alaska. It is a dry, hard cracker that can be stored for a long time.

FERN FIDDLEHEADS

Fiddleheads are the coiled-up tips of young Ostrich Ferns and Lady Ferns, two types of ferns found in Alaska. They are often foraged in the spring and then roasted, steamed, or boiled. Please note: not all ferns are edible and once fiddleheads are uncoiled, they can no longer be eaten.

ESKIMO ICE CREAM

Also known as Akutuk or akutaq, this is a traditional Alaskan dessert made by mixing together whipped fat (such as reindeer or seal oil) with berries and sometimes sugar. Other common ingredients include ground fish, tundra greens, and boiled and mashed potatoes. The mixture is whipped until it reaches a light and fluffy consistency, similar to buttercream frosting.

It is a beloved treat in many Alaska Native communities and is often served at celebrations and feasts.

. . .

KELP PICKLES

Made from ocean-grown bull kelp and infused with dill, spices and brine, kelp pickles are an Alaskan treat.

KELP SALSA

A tangy and salty salsa made from kelp, which is abundant in Alaska's coastal waters.

MORE KELP CUISINE

In Alaska, you'll find a few more unique kelp food items such as kelp pesto, kelp hot sauce, and kelp smoothies.

MAKTAK

Maktak is a traditional Inuit and Chukchi food, made from the fatty outer layer of whale skin, usually from bowhead whales. It's usually eaten raw, but can also be eaten frozen, cooked, deep-fried, dipped in soy sauce or pickled. Maktak can be both chewy and tender, meaty and oily, and can taste slightly fishy to nutty. However you eat it, maktak is a pure Alaskan treat and is considered a delicacy.

MUKTUK

Muktuk is a traditional Inuit food that consists of whale skin and blubber. It is a high-protein, high-fat food typically served raw or pickled, and it is a significant part of the traditional Inuit diet.

Muktuk is often considered a delicacy and is eaten on special occasions and celebrations. It has a chewy texture and a slightly fishy flavor.

MAKTAK & MUKTUK: NOT THE SAME

Maktak and muktuk are similar, but they are not exactly the same thing. Maktak is a traditional Inuit and Yupik food made from the fatty layer of whale skin, while muktuk typically refers to the skin and blubber of the whale, usually the beluga or bowhead whale.

Both are traditional foods in Alaska and other parts of the Arctic, and are often eaten raw or pickled.

KING CRAB

Alaska is famous for its king crab, which is harvested from the waters of the Bering Sea and the Gulf of Alaska. It is known for its sweet and succulent meat.

SALMON

Alaska is known for its wild salmon, which is served in a variety of ways, such as smoked, grilled, or baked.

. . .

HALIBUT

Halibut is a popular fish in Alaska and is known for its firm, white flesh and delicate flavor.

MOOSE, REINDEER, AND CARIBOU

These are common and essential meats for many Alaska Natives and often made into burgers, sausages, stews, and jerky.

17

INTERESTING WAR HISTORY

Alaska has a unique war history that is often overlooked. During World War II, Alaska became a battleground as the Japanese attempted to invade the state and gain a foothold in North America. The state's strategic location and rich resources made it a target, and the US military worked to defend the state and drive the Japanese back.

ALASKA WAS INVADED BY THE JAPANESE IN WORLD WAR II

The Battle of Attu: In June 1942, the Japanese invaded the Aleutian Islands and seized the islands of Attu and Kiska. US forces launched a counterattack, and the Battle of Attu became one of the deadliest battles of the Pacific campaign. The battle lasted for nearly three weeks, and in total about 4,000 combatants were killed or wounded.

. . .

PRISONERS OF WAR

In 1942, when the Japanese invaded, the residents of Attu village were taken prisoner by the Japanese and transported back to Hokkaido, where they remained until the end of the war in 1945.

THE ALASKA HIGHWAY

The US military built the Alaska Highway during World War II to connect Alaska, through western Canada, with the rest of the United States. The 1,500-mile (2,414 km) highway was built in just eight months and was a remarkable feat of engineering. The highway provided a critical supply line for the military and also helped to open up Alaska to tourism and economic development.

THE ALASKA SCOUTS

The US military recruited Alaska Natives to serve as scouts and guides during the war. The Alaska Scouts played a crucial role in reconnaissance and intelligence gathering, as they knew the terrain and weather conditions better than any other soldiers. They were expert hunters, trackers, and survivalists who were well-suited to the harsh environment of Alaska.

THE ALASKA TERRITORIAL GUARD

In response to the threat of a Japanese invasion, the US military organized the Alaska Territorial Guard (ATG), a Native Alaskan force that patrolled the coastline and served as an early warning system. The ATG was the only military unit in US history composed entirely of Indigenous soldiers. Although they were not initially paid or recognized for their service, the ATG played a critical role in the defense of Alaska during the war.

THE COLD WAR

After World War II, Alaska continued to play a strategic role in national defense as tensions between the US and the Soviet Union escalated. Alaska was home to numerous military bases and installations, including the massive Elmendorf Air Force Base and Fort Richardson. These bases served as a critical deterrent against Soviet aggression and helped to protect the US from potential attack.

18

ALASKA'S GOLD RUSH

The Alaska Gold Rush, also known as the Klondike Gold Rush, was a period of frenzied gold prospecting and mining activity in Alaska and the Yukon territory of Canada in the late 1800s and early 1900s.

GOLD! THERE BE GOLD IN ALASKA

The Alaska Gold Rush began in 1896, when gold was discovered in the Klondike region of Canada, near the Alaska border. The discovery set off a stampede of prospectors who traveled to the area in search of fortune.

WHY IT'S CALLED THE KLONDIKE GOLD RUSH

The Klondike Gold Rush is named after the Klondike River in the Klondike region, which is located in the Yukon Territory in the northwestern part of Canada, near the border with Alaska. The Klondike River and surrounding creeks and tributaries proved to be some of the richest sources of gold in the region.

MASSIVE GOLD NUGGETS

Some of the largest gold nuggets ever found were discovered during this time. The largest nugget found in Yukon weighed over 72 ounces, or 4.5 pounds (2.04 kg)!

POTATOES USED AS CURRENCY

Potatoes were very valuable during the gold rush because they helped prevent scurvy, a disease caused by a lack of vitamin C. Fresh fruits and vegetables were scarce in the Klondike, and potatoes were one of the few vegetables that could be grown locally. Miners would sometimes trade potatoes for other goods or services.

GOLD DISCOVERED EARLIER

The first gold "discovery" in Alaska itself is generally attributed to a man named Joseph Juneau, who, along with Richard Harris, found gold in what is now known as Gold Creek in Southeast Alaska in 1880. The city of Juneau, later founded in the area, was named after Joseph Juneau.

GOLD WASN'T NEW TO ALASKA NATIVES

The Indigenous peoples in Alaska had long known about and valued gold, and had used it for both decorative and ceremonial purposes. Gold was also used in trade and exchange between Indigenous groups and with other cultures, including Russian traders who had established a presence in Alaska during the 18th and 19th centuries. So, while Juneau is often credited with the "discovery" of gold in Alaska, it's important to recognize that gold had a long history in the region prior to his arrival.

PEOPLE STILL FIND GOLD IN ALASKA TODAY

While the large, easily accessible gold deposits discovered during the gold rush days have since been depleted, smaller deposits of gold remain scattered throughout the state.

Recreational gold panning is a popular activity in Alaska, and many visitors come to the state to try their hand at finding gold. There are even businesses that offer guided gold-panning tours, where visitors can learn about gold rush history and try their luck at finding gold in a controlled setting.

In addition to recreational gold panning, there are still some commercial gold mining operations in Alaska.

Famous Characters from the Klondike Gold Rush

GEORGE CARMACK

Carmack was a prospector who, along with Skookum Jim and his brothers-in-law, made the first gold strike in the Klondike.

He later became a successful miner and businessman, and his name is forever associated with the history of the Yukon Gold Rush.

SKOOKUM JIM MASON

Skookum Jim was a Tagish First Nation man who helped lead the first gold strike in the Klondike. He and his cousins, George and Dawson Charlie, discovered the first large nuggets of gold in Rabbit Creek (later renamed Bonanza Creek) in 1896, which triggered the Klondike Gold Rush.

JACK LONDON

The famous American author traveled to the Klondike in 1897 in search of gold, but returned empty-handed. His experiences in the North, however, inspired some of his most famous works, including *The Call of the Wild* and *White Fang*.

SOAPY SMITH

Jefferson Randolph "Soapy" Smith was a notorious con artist and gang leader who operated in the Klondike during the gold rush. He ran a number of scams and illicit operations, including a rigged gambling house, and became one of the most infamous figures of the time.

He was challenged to a shootout by a man named Frank Reid, who led a group of vigilantes. The shootout is known as the

"Shootout on Juneau Wharf." Both men were mortally wounded in the exchange, and Smith died on the spot.

BELINDA MULROONEY

Mulrooney was a successful businesswoman and entrepreneur who ran a number of ventures in the Klondike, including a boarding house, a restaurant, and a saloon. She became one of the wealthiest people in the region, and her story is often cited as an example of the opportunities the gold rush presented to women.

WYATT EARP

Wyatt Earp is best known for his role as a lawman in the American West, particularly in the town of Tombstone, Arizona. In 1897, Wyatt Earp traveled to Alaska with a partner named Charlie Hoxie to prospect for gold. After unsuccessful attempts in Nome, they settled in St. Michael, where they established a saloon and gambling hall called the Dexter that catered to miners and travelers.

Earp's time in Alaska was relatively successful, but he also faced legal trouble when he was arrested for assault and battery after a dispute with a fellow saloon owner in 1899. Despite the incident, Earp made a name for himself in the region and is remembered as a colorful character who was involved in the Klondike Gold Rush.

19

FILMED IN ALASKA

Movies Filmed in Alaska

Turns out, while there are many movies set in Alaska, a lot of them aren't actually filmed in Alaska. Here are a few that were:

ALASKA (1996)

The 1996 adventure film *Alaska* tells the story of two children, Jessie and her younger brother Sean, who travel to Alaska with their father, a bush pilot named Jake Barnes. After their plane crashes in the wilderness, the three are forced to work together to survive against the harsh and unforgiving Alaskan wilderness.

While some scenes were filmed on location in Alaska, the majority of the film was shot in British Columbia, Canada.

. . .

THE EDGE (1997)

The Edge is a 1997 film about a billionaire, a photographer and a journalist who are stranded in the wilderness of Alaska after their plane crashes. The group must survive in the harsh wilderness and overcome their personal differences as they try to find their way back to civilization.

The film was mostly made in British Columbia, but some scenes were filmed in Alaska.

INTO THE WILD (2007)

Into the Wild is a movie directed by Sean Penn, based on the true story of Christopher McCandless, a young man who sets out on a journey to Alaska in search of adventure and self-discovery. McCandless ventures into the Alaskan wilderness with the goal of living off the land. However, as he struggles to survive, he realizes that he may have underestimated the harshness of the environment.

The film was primarily filmed in the state of Alaska, with locations including Healy, Cantwell, and Denali National Park.

THE PROPOSAL (2009)

The Proposal is a romantic comedy film released in 2009. It stars Sandra Bullock as Margaret Tate, a demanding and powerful book editor, and Ryan Reynolds as Andrew Paxton, her assistant. Margaret is about to be deported to Canada, so she convinces Andrew to pretend to be her fiancé to help her stay in the US. They travel to Andrew's hometown in Alaska, where they meet his family and face a series of challenges as they try to keep up the pretense of their engagement.

Most of *The Proposal* was filmed in Massachusetts and New England, but some scenes were filmed in Alaska, including the location of Andrew's hometown.

BIG MIRACLE (2012)

Big Miracle is a 2012 movie based on the true story of a reporter and a Greenpeace volunteer who team up to save a family of whales trapped in ice in Alaska in 1988.

The film was shot in various locations in Alaska, including Anchorage, Barrow, and the nearby Arctic National Wildlife Refuge.

MOVIES SET IN ALASKA, BUT NOT FILMED IN ALASKA

While it may seem like these movies were filmed in Alaska, they were not. How many of these did you think were filmed in Alaska?

- *Insomnia* (2002) – A psychological crime thriller directed by Christopher Nolan. It was primarily filmed in Vancouver and Kamloops, British Columbia, Canada, with some scenes filmed in Tromsø, Norway. Though set in Alaska, there is no information to suggest that any part of the movie was filmed there.

- **The Guardian** (2006) – Set in Alaska but filmed in British Columbia.
- **Snow Dogs** (2002) – Set in Alaska but filmed in British Columbia.
- **A Killing in a Small Town** (1990) – Set in Alaska but filmed in British Columbia.
- **The Snow Walker** (2003) is a Canadian film set in the 1950s, which follows the journey of a pilot and his passenger who crash in the remote wilderness of Alaska. The film was shot in various locations in Canada, including British Columbia, and not in Alaska.
- **The Fourth Kind** (2009) is a science-fiction horror film that takes place in Nome, Alaska. The movie was filmed in Bulgaria and Morocco, not in Alaska.
- **Mystery, Alaska** (1991) is a sports comedy-drama film set in the fictional small town of Mystery, Alaska. The film was primarily shot in the Bow Valley of Alberta, not in Alaska.
- **White Fang** (1991) – Based on the classic novel by Jack London, it tells the story of a young gold prospector, Jack Conroy, and his adventures in the Alaskan wilderness with a half-wolf, half-dog named White Fang. The movie was filmed in British Columbia.

TV Shows Filmed in Alaska

DEADLIEST CATCH (2005–)

A documentary-style reality TV show that follows the lives of crab fishermen working in the dangerous waters of the Bering Sea off the coast of Alaska. The show, which first aired in 2005, is filmed on location in the Bering Sea and in the port city of Dutch Harbor in the Aleutian Islands, Alaska.

GOLD RUSH (2010–)

Gold Rush is a reality TV show about gold mining in Alaska. The show is primarily filmed in Alaska, where the miners brave harsh weather conditions and challenging terrain to try to strike it rich.

PIRATE GOLD OF ADAK ISLAND (2022–)

Pirate Gold of Adak Island is a reality TV series that follows a team of treasure hunters as they search for a rumored $300 million in gold that is said to be buried on Adak Island in Alaska. The island is located in the Bering Sea, about 1,500 miles southwest of Anchorage.

BERING SEA GOLD (2012–)

A reality-TV show that follows gold miners based in Nome, Alaska, as they search for gold in the Bering Sea. The show highlights the dangerous and challenging work of gold mining,

as well as the miners' personal lives and relationships. The
show was filmed in Nome.

ALASKA: THE LAST FRONTIER (2011–)

Centering on the lives of the Kilcher family, who live on a
homestead near Homer, Alaska, the show documents their
daily lives, including their subsistence lifestyle and their work
to maintain the homestead, which includes hunting, fishing,
and farming. The show was filmed on the Kilcher family's
homestead in Alaska.

LIFE BELOW ZERO (2013–)

A reality-TV show that follows the lives of several individuals
who live off the grid in remote parts of Alaska. The show showcases the challenges and triumphs of life in one of the harshest
environments in the world, where the residents must rely on
their own survival skills and ingenuity to thrive. It was filmed
in various locations throughout Alaska, including the Brooks
Range, the North Slope, and the Aleutian Islands.

ICE ROAD TRUCKERS (2007–2017)

Showcasing specialized truck drivers as they transport goods
over frozen lakes and rivers in remote areas of Alaska, the show
highlights the dangerous and challenging conditions the
truckers face, including thin ice, harsh weather, and unpredictable terrain. The show was filmed primarily in Alaska, with
some scenes filmed in Canada's Northwest Territories.

· · ·

THE LAST ALASKANS (2015–)

Focused on the lives of people living in the Arctic National Wildlife Refuge in Alaska, the show explores the relationships, challenges, and unique lifestyles of the residents, who are among the few people living in the refuge. The show was filmed in the Arctic National Wildlife Refuge in Alaska.

FLYING WILD ALASKA (2011–2012)

A reality-TV show that followed the Tweto family, who owned and operated Alaska's largest regional airline, Era Alaska. The show followed the family as they flew passengers and cargo to remote Alaskan villages, braved severe weather conditions, and dealt with the challenges of running a successful business in Alaska's rugged wilderness. The show was filmed in various locations across Alaska, including Unalakleet, Nome, Kotzebue, and other small Alaskan communities.

EDGE OF ALASKA (2014–2017)

Focused on the town of McCarthy and its residents, who work to maintain their way of life while facing challenges such as harsh weather and limited resources, the show was filmed on location in McCarthy, Alaska, in the Wrangell-St. Elias National Park and Preserve.

ALASKA STATE TROOPERS (2009–)

A reality-TV show that follows the daily operations of the Alaska State Troopers, a law enforcement agency responsible for maintaining order and enforcing state laws in Alaska. The show is filmed across various locations in Alaska, including rural communities, wilderness areas, and cities. The program highlights the challenges faced by the troopers in serving and protecting the state's vast and diverse geography, and showcases their work in rescuing lost hikers, apprehending criminals, and responding to emergency situations.

TV SHOWS SET IN ALASKA, BUT NOT FILMED IN ALASKA

There are a few television shows that were set in Alaska, but not actually filmed there. A few examples include:

- *Northern Exposure* (1990–1995): set in the fictional town of Cicely, Alaska, but filmed in Roslyn, Washington.
- *The Twilight Zone* (1959–1964): One episode, "The Hunt," is set in Alaska and features a dog sled team being pursued by a pack of wolves, but it was not filmed in Alaska.

DID YOU KNOW?

The *FV Aleutian Ballad*, a fishing vessel that was featured on the Discovery Channel show *Deadliest Catch*, is now a tour boat in Ketchikan. The boat teaches people about the fishing, crabbing, prawning, and other industries in Alaska. It also showcases the bald eagles that are abundant in the area.

20

FAMOUS ALASKANS

Movie & TV Stars

IRENE BEDARD

Born in Anchorage and a Native Alaskan, Bedard is best known for her speaking voice in Disney's animated film Pocahontas (1995).

She is also known for her roles in films and television series such as *Smoke Signals*, *The Sopranos*, and *Into the West*.

DARBY STANCHFIELD

She was born in Kodiak, Alaska, and is best known for her role in Shonda Rhimes' hit show *Scandal*. Her father was a commercial fisherman in Alaska, and Darby has said, "What I miss most about living in Alaska is the fishing."

· · ·

DON SIMPSON

He co-produced some major films with his partner Jerry Bruck-heimer, including *Flashdance* (1983), *Beverly Hills Cop* (1984), *Top Gun* (1986), and *The Rock* (1996). While Simpson was not born in Alaska, he grew up in Juneau.

Famous Musicians

JEWEL

Born in Utah as Jewel Kilcher, she was raised not far from Homer, Alaska. The singer-songwriter, actress and author had sold over 30 million albums worldwide as of 2021.

When she lived outside of Homer, her family had no running water, no heat—just a coal stove and an outhouse. They mostly lived off of what they could kill or preserve. They picked berries and made jam. They caught fish to freeze, kept a garden, and raised cattle. She loved it.

PORTUGAL. THE MAN

Portugal. The Man is an American rock band formed in Wasilla, Alaska, in 2004. The band consists of John Gourley (vocals, guitar), Zach Carothers (bass), Kyle O'Quin (keyboard), Eric Howk (guitar) and Jason Sechrist (drums). They are best known for their hit single "Feel It Still," which topped charts and won the Grammy for Best Pop Duo/Group Performance in

2018. The band's musical style combines elements of psychedelic rock, pop, and electronic music.

Famous Alaskan Authors

JOHN HAINES, POET

John Haines was an American poet and essayist associated with the "Alaska School" of poetry. He lived in Alaska for many years, and his work often reflects his experiences in the Alaskan wilderness. Haines is considered one of the most important poets of the 20th century, and his work has been widely published.

JOAN DIDION, WRITER AND JOURNALIST

Joan Didion was an American writer and journalist known for her essays, novels, and screenplays. She was considered a prominent figure in contemporary American literature and won several awards for her work. Didion's writing often explored themes of personal and cultural identity, politics, and morality. Some of her most famous works include *Slouching Towards Bethlehem, The White Album*, and *The Year of Magical Thinking*.

SHERRY SIMPSON, WRITER AND EDITOR

Sherry Simpson is an American writer and editor from Alaska. She is known for her work as a journalist, memoirist, and fiction writer, and has written extensively about Alaska's landscape, people, and history.

Simpson is the author of several books, including *The Way Winter Comes, The Accidental Explorer*, and *Dancing on the Edge of the World*. She has received numerous awards for her writing, including the Alaska Governor's Award for the Arts and the Pushcart Prize.

DAVID VANN, WRITER

David Vann is an American writer, best known for his works of fiction that often draw upon his experiences growing up in Alaska and his family history. He is the author of several novels and essay collections, including the award-winning memoir, *A Mile Down: The True Story of a Disastrous Career at Sea*. Vann's writing style is often described as dark and introspective, exploring themes of family, loss, and the human experience.

NANCY LORD, WRITER, ESSAYIST AND POET

Nancy Lord is an Alaskan author, essayist, and poet who has written extensively about Alaska and the Pacific Northwest. She is best known for her essays and stories that explore the people and cultures of Alaska, including Indigenous communities and the state's diverse landscape.

Lord has published several collections of essays and poems, including *Early NW Coastal Indian Life: The Wrangell Coop-*

erative Report, Beluga Days: Tracking the Mystery of Alaska's White Whales, and *Green Alaska: Dreams from the Far Coast*.

PEGGY SHUMAKER, WRITER AND POET

Peggy Shumaker is an American poet and writer. She was born in California in 1947 and grew up in Alaska. She has published several books of poetry and creative nonfiction that often focus on her experiences in Alaska and her relationship with the natural world. She is a professor emerita of creative writing at the University of Alaska Fairbanks and has received numerous awards and honors for her writing, including the Washington State Governor's Award for Literature.

SETH KANTNER, WRITER AND JOURNALIST

Seth Kantner is an Alaskan author and journalist best known for his non-fiction writing about life in the Alaskan wilderness and the Indigenous people of the region. He is the author of the books *Ordinary Wolves* and *Shopping for Porcupine*. His writing focuses on the relationships between people and the natural world and the struggle to maintain a connection to the land in modern times.

RICHARD JAMES PROENNEKE, WRITER, NATURALIST AND FILMMAKER

Richard James Proenneke was a naturalist, author, and film-maker, best known for his journal and book *One Man's Wilderness: An Alaskan Odyssey*, documenting his life in the wilderness of Alaska. The book, published in 1999, is based on the notes and recordings Proenneke made during his 30-year stay in the Alaskan wilderness, where he built a log cabin and lived a self-sufficient life. Proenneke is considered an important figure in the history of Alaskan wilderness living and survival.

DOUGLAS J. EBOCH, SCREENWRITER

Eboch grew up in Juneau and is best known for screenwriting the 2002 film Sweet Home Alabama. He also wrote the video game *Night Cove* and the children's Christmas play called *Sleepover at the Stable*.

JACK LONDON, WRITER

While not born in Alaska, two of his best-selling and well-known works are based in Alaska. At the age of 21, London travelled to Nome, Alaska, during the Klondike Gold Rush to find his fortune. While he didn't find gold, he did find the inspiration for two of the all-time best-known novels based in Alaska.

You may have heard of *The Call of the Wild* and *White Fang*. *The Call of the Wild* has been translated into almost 100 languages and made into movie staring Harrison Ford. These works helped to popularize Alaska and gave readers around the world a glimpse into life in the frontier territory.

21

ALASKAN SUPERSTITIONS, MYTHS & MYSTERIOUS CREATURES

SPECIAL NOTE FROM THE AUTHOR

There are many Native Alaskan stories and beliefs that I have come across as part of the research for this section.

Whilst stories on folklore and superstitions have been included, I have specifically chosen not to include Native Alaskan stories on cultural learnings, sacred beliefs and teachings out of respect for the Indigenous communities. These are not my stories to tell.

To learn more about Native Alaskan storytelling, please visit the Alaska Native Heritage Center website: https://www.alaskanative.net/

COMMON ALASKAN SUPERSTITIONS

- Stepping on a crack in the ice will bring bad luck.

- Pointing at the Northern Lights will bring them closer but will also anger them and make them disappear.
- Whistling in a kayak will summon strong winds.
- Catching a fish with your bare hands will bring good luck.
- If a whale breaches next to a fishing boat, it means a big catch is coming.
- Breaking a fishing line means a bad day on the water.

THE ALASKA TRIANGLE MYTH

The Alaska Triangle, also known as the Devil's Triangle, is a region in Alaska where a large number of planes and ships have disappeared under supposedly mysterious circumstances.

Similar to the Bermuda Triangle, it is often believed that the Alaska Triangle is cursed or haunted, and that strange, supernatural forces are at work there. Some say that the disappearances are due to the rugged, remote terrain and harsh weather conditions, while others attribute them to powerful and unpredictable forces of nature, such as magnetic anomalies or even alien activity.

Two of the most famous disappearances within the Alaskan Triangle include:

- The vanishing of a C-54 Skymaster military aircraft, carrying eight crew members and 36 passengers.

- The disappearance of an aircraft carrying the 1972 US House Majority Leader Hale Boggs.

As of 2023, no trace of either aircraft was ever found.

Despite the many theories and legends surrounding the Alaska Triangle, there is no scientific evidence to support the idea that it is a dangerous or cursed area. Nevertheless, the many unsolved mysteries in the region continue to captivate the imagination of people around the world.

ALASKA'S LOCH NESS MONSTER, "ILLIE"

Illie is a legendary creature said to inhabit the waters of Iliamna Lake in Alaska. It is often described as a large, serpentine or eel-like creature anywhere from 10 to 30 feet long. There have been numerous reported sightings of Illie over the years, although there is no conclusive scientific evidence of its existence.

Despite the lack of concrete evidence, Illie is a popular topic of conversation and has become something of a local legend. Some locals claim to have seen Illie firsthand, while others believe the creature is a myth or a figment of people's imaginations.

In any case, Illie has become an important part of Alaska's folklore and continues to be a subject of fascination for many people.

. . .

ALASKA'S VERSION OF BIGFOOT: THE BUSHMAN OR TORNIT

According to Alaska Native legend, the Tornit (also known as the Bushman) is a creature that inhabits the wilds of Alaska. The Tornit is often described as a large, hairy humanoid that resembles the better-known Bigfoot, or Sasquatch. However, unlike Bigfoot, the Tornit is said to be aggressive and territorial, and to attack humans who venture too close to its territory.

AI rendering of Alaska's version of Bigfoot by the author via Midjourney.

The legend of the Tornit has been passed down through generations of Alaska Native communities, particularly among the Inuit and Yupik peoples. It is said the Tornit lives in remote areas of the tundra and forests, and is capable of communicating with humans using a primitive language.

.   .   .

THE KUSHTAKA, NOT YOUR GARDEN-VARIETY SEA OTTER

The Kushtaka is a creature from the Tlingit and Tsimshian peoples of Southeast Alaska. The Kushtaka is often described as a shapeshifting otter-man or otter-woman that can take on a human form to lure people to their deaths.

The Kushtaka is known for imitating the cries of a baby or the screams of a drowning person to lure people to the water's edge. Once the victim is within reach, the Kushtaka drags them into the water, never to be seen again. The Kushtaka is also believed to have the power to confuse and disorient people, leading them to become lost in the wilderness.

To avoid being lured by the Kushtaka, one is advised to avoid the water's edge when hearing strange sounds, or to carry a knife or another sharp object as protection.

THE ADLET, HALF-HUMAN, HALF-DOG

The Inuit tell of the Adlet, creature that is half-human and half-dog. The story goes that a woman was kidnapped by a pack of dogs, and when she returned to her village, she gave birth to ten children who were half-human, half-dog. These children were called Adlet, and they were known for their fierce strength and hunting ability.

The Adlet were banished to an island where they lived in solitude for many years. But as time went on, they grew restless and wanted to rejoin their human ancestors. They built a boat and set out to sea, but when they arrived on the mainland, they were met with hostility and fear from the humans.

Despite this, the Adlet persisted and eventually integrated into human society. They were known for their incredible physical abilities and were often hired as hunters or warriors. However, their unique appearance and origin story also made them outsiders, and they were often treated with suspicion and fear.

Today, the Adlet are considered a symbol of resilience and strength in Inuit culture, and their story continues to be told and celebrated.

IRCENRRAAT, THE "LITTLE PEOPLE" OF ALASKA

The Irish aren't the only ones who have stories about little people. Ircenrraat, also known as "little people," are creatures described in Yup'ik stories, said to be small, mischievous beings that live in the tundra and taiga regions of Alaska. They have the ability to make themselves invisible and can control the weather.

It is said that if a person sees an Ircenrraat, they may become sick or be struck with bad luck. To protect oneself from them, offerings such as small pieces of food or toys are left outside to appease the Ircenrraat and prevent them from causing harm.

. . .

Some legends also suggest that Ircenrraat can help humans in times of need, such as finding lost objects or guiding travelers through treacherous terrain. Despite their reputation as mischievous beings, they are sometimes depicted as helpful and friendly, especially towards children.

KATS, THE HALF-MAN, HALF-BEAR

Kats is a half-man, half-bear creature described in stories of the Tlingit people of Alaska. Kats is said to have been created by a woman who married a bear, and their offspring became the first Kats. These creatures are powerful and feared, possessing the strength and ferocity of a bear, as well as the intelligence and ingenuity of a human.

Kats can shape-shift at will, taking on the form of a human or a bear, or even something in between. They are known for their incredible hunting skills and their ability to move through the forest undetected. Some stories also suggest that Kats have magical powers, including the ability to control the weather and communicate with animals.

Despite their fearsome reputation, Kats are said to be protective of their families and their territory, and they will only attack humans if provoked. They are also considered to be guardians of the forest and the animals that live there, and are often associated with the natural world and the balance of nature.

22

ALASKA'S FAMOUS ATTRACTIONS & UNIQUE FESTIVALS

THE WHALE BONE ARCHES

The Whale Bone Arches in the city of Utqiaġvik, formally known as Barrow, Alaska. Photo by Dewhurst Donna, U.S. Fish and Wildlife Service, Public Domain.

The Whale Bone Arches are a landmark in the city of Barrow, now called Utqiaġvik. They are two large arches made from the bones of bowhead whales that have been used as a symbol of the Inupiaq culture for centuries. The arches are located near the entrance to Barrow Beach and are one of the most famous tourist attractions in the city. The arches are a reminder of the importance of hunting and subsistence living to the Inupiaq people and their close relationship with the land and sea.

THE AURORA ICE MUSEUM

The Aurora Ice Museum is a unique attraction located in Chena Hot Springs. It's built entirely of ice and showcases various ice sculptures, ice carvings and ice chandeliers. The museum offers visitors a one-of-a-kind opportunity to walk through a winter wonderland, complete with ice slides and ice bars serving drinks.

UPSIDE DOWN TREE GARDEN

The Upside Down Tree Garden in Glacier Gardens is a fascinating sight in Juneau. It features a variety of trees that have been uprooted and replanted upside down, their root systems forming a sort of natural flower pot for floral displays, creating an interesting sight. Visitors can explore the garden, take photos, and soak in the amazing views of the surrounding area.

THE HAMMER MUSEUM IN HAINES

The Hammer Museum in Haines is dedicated to the history of hammers. It showcases an extensive collection of hammers and other hand tools, including early hand-forged iron hammers, vintage carpenters' hammers, and modern power hammers. The museum also features exhibits on the evolution of hammer design and the various techniques and tools used in black-smithing.

SPIRIT HOUSES

Traditional Athabaskan spirit houses built to mark the graves of deceased loved ones. Photo by Jeffrey Beall via Flickr (CC by ND-2.0).

Spirit houses are a traditional Athabaskan practice in Alaska. These small wooden structures are built to mark the graves and honor the spirits of deceased ancestors and loved ones. They often contain offerings such as food, tobacco, or other items meant to reflect the passed loved one and ensure their well-being in the afterlife. Spirit houses are considered sacred and are a way of maintaining a connection with the spirits of the dead.

Spirit houses are a unique part of Alaskan culture, and can be found throughout the state. They are often placed near fishing areas, rivers, and mountains. Some of the best-known collections of spirit houses are located in Anchorage, Fairbanks, and Juneau. It's important to be respectful and keep a distance, remembering the spiritual significance of these places.

Spirt houses outside the St. Nicholas Orthodox Church in Eklutna, Alaska. Photo by Kasia Halka via Flickr.

ICE CAVES

Ice caves in Alaska. Photo by Paxson Woelber on Unsplash.

There are several ice caves open to visitors in Alaska. One of the most popular is in the Mendenhall Glacier in Juneau. Other popular ice caves include Glacier Bay, Matanuska Glacier, Exit Glacier, and Tustumena Glacier. If you're looking for more adventure, you can explore some of the lesser-known ice caves, like the Blue Glacier in the Chugach Mountains, or the Spencer Glacier in the Kenai Fjords National Park.

MENDENHALL GLACIER

The Mendenhall Glacier in Juneau is home to a famous network of ice caves that visitors can explore. The caves are formed as the glacier melts, revealing deep blue caverns within the ice. To visit, one typically takes a guided tour, as the caves can be unstable and dangerous to enter without proper knowledge and equipment.

WHITTIER, THE TOWN UNDER ONE ROOF

Whittier is a city in the Prince William Sound region of Alaska where the majority of the population lives in one building, known as the Begich Towers. This building serves as a housing complex, community center, and transportation hub for the roughly 220 residents. It was built in the 1950s to serve as a military housing during the Cold War and later became a civilian housing complex.

The building is a unique example of the extreme living conditions in Alaska, and its history reflects the state's political and social changes over the years.

. . .

GOLDEN DAYS

Golden Days is a celebration that takes place Fairbanks during the second week of July. It is a week-long celebration that marks the discovery of gold in the Fairbanks area in 1902. The celebration features a variety of events, including parades, live music, food vendors, historical reenactments, and more. The highlight of Golden Days is the Discovery Days parade, one of the largest parades in Alaska, which features floats, marching bands, and other participants celebrating the city's gold rush heritage.

MOOSE DROPPINGS FESTIVAL IN TALKEETNA

The Moose Droppings Festival is a yearly event in Talkeetna that takes place in late August. It features live music, local food, arts and crafts, and a variety of outdoor activities and games. The festival also includes a variety of contests, such as a moose calling contest and one where participants try to guess the weight of a large block of moose droppings, with the winner receiving a cash prize. The festival is a unique and quirky celebration of Alaskan culture and humor that attracts visitors from all over the state and beyond.

THE LITTLE NORWAY FESTIVAL

The Little Norway Festival is a cultural celebration that takes place annually in Petersburg, Alaska, usually in the summer. It is a celebration of the Norwegian heritage in Alaska and features traditional Norwegian food, music, and dance. The festival also showcases traditional Norwegian costumes and arts and crafts, and there are usually demonstrations of traditional skills such as wood carving and lace making. The festival is a celebration of the long history of Norwegian settlement in Alaska, and provides an opportunity for the community to come together to celebrate their heritage and traditions.

RUBBER DUCKY FESTIVAL

Hundreds of rubber duckies.

Alaska's Rubber Ducky Festival is an annual event held on the second Saturday of June in Juneau. Every summer, locals and visitors alike gather to celebrate the rubber ducky, a beloved city mascot. The festival includes a rubber ducky parade, games, contests, a rubber ducky race, and much more.

THE GREAT BATHTUB RACE

The Great Bathtub Race is an annual event held during the summer in Nome, Alaska. Participants line up at High Noon and race bathtubs 100 yards (0.9 meters) down Front Street in downtown Nome.

An example of a bathtub on wheels used to race in the The Great Bathtub Race in Nome, Alaska. Photo by David Okitkon via Flickr.

Teams are made up of five people, with one of the team members inside the tub, while the other four push the tub, which is mounted on wheels, down the street to the finish line. Each member is required to carry one of four items, a large bar of soap, a washcloth, a bath towel, and a bath mat. The team captain inside the tub, is encouraged to pretend like they're taking a bath. At the start of the race, the bathtub must be full of water. By the end, it must have at least 10 gallons of water still in the tub!

. . .

Prizes include bragging rights and a unique trophy that is passed down each year from winner to winner. This unusual trophy is a figurine of Kermit and Miss Piggy taking a bath.

SITKA MERMAID FESTIVAL

The Sitka Mermaid Festival is an annual event in Sitka that celebrates the area's unique connection to the ocean. It includes a parade, live music, food vendors, arts and crafts, and other events. A main feature of the festival is the mermaid parade, where participants dress up in elaborate mermaid costumes and march through the streets of Sitka.

CORDOVA ICEWORM FESTIVAL

This annual festival takes place in Cordova in February. It celebrates ice worms, which live and breed in the glaciers. The festival features a parade, live music, contests, and other activities for visitors, as well as a candlelight snowshoe hike to the glaciers to observe the ice worms, which are bioluminescent and emit a bright blue light.

HOMER HIGHLAND GAMES

The Homer Highland Games is an annual festival held in Homer that celebrates Scottish and Celtic culture. The festival typically features traditional Scottish athletic competitions, such as caber tossing and stone putting, as well as live music, dancing, and food vendors.

23

WAYS TO SEE & EXPLORE ALASKA

Alaska By Cruise Ship

Alaska is one of the top five cruise destinations for US travelers. Over a million passengers see Alaska by cruise ship. Many cruise lines offer Alaskan itineraries that typically last 7–14 days. Passengers can enjoy scenic views of glaciers, fjords, and wildlife, as well as visit various ports of call.

Some popular destinations for tourists visiting Alaska by cruise include the cities of Juneau, Ketchikan, and Skagway, and the glaciers of Glacier Bay National Park.

In addition to scenic sightseeing, many cruise ships also offer onboard activities and excursions such as whale watching, dog sledding, and fishing.

. . .

CRUISE SHIP SIGHTINGS

Locals consider the first cruise ship appearance in the Alaska harbors to be the start to the busy tourist season. The Alaska cruise season runs from late April to early September, covering spring, summer, and autumn. The peak season is from June to September, with May and October having fewer cruises. Each season has its pros and cons, such as weather, wildlife, cost, and crowds. The busiest time is typically June to August.

PEOPLE HAVE BEEN CRUISING TO ALASKA FOR OVER A CENTURY

People have been coming to visit Alaska by cruise ship for more than a century. Cruising to Alaska started with Pacific Coast Steamship Co. of San Francisco in the 1880s.

2023 CRUISE SHIP VISITORS

Some 41 cruise ships, making 694 calls to port, were expected for the 2023 season, with 1.3 million visitors expected to arrive by cruise ship. This included huge cruise ships like *Quantum of the Seas*, with a maximum capacity of 6,680 passengers, and smaller ships like the *Windstar Star Breeze*, accommodating 312 guests.

THE THREE BUSIEST PORTS

Juneau, Ketchikan and Skagway are the most popular and busiest ports, with over 80 percent of all cruise passenger visits to Alaska.

. . .

THREE MAIN CRUISE ROUTES

There are three basic routes to see Alaska. They include:

- **Inside Passage:** This route is the most popular and takes passengers through the scenic Inside Passage, a protected waterway that runs along the coast of Alaska and British Columbia. It is known for its stunning views of glaciers, fjords, and wildlife, and stops at ports like Ketchikan, Juneau, and Skagway.
- **Gulf of Alaska:** This route travels along the open waters of the Gulf of Alaska and offers a more rugged and remote experience. It stops at ports like Whittier, Valdez, and Seward, and provides the opportunity to see glaciers and wildlife up close.
- **Bering Strait:** The Bering Strait is a narrow waterway that separates Alaska and Russia, and some cruise lines offer voyages that cross this strait and explore the remote and pristine wilderness of the Arctic. These cruises are typically more adventurous and typically cater to more experienced travelers, as they offer the opportunity to see remote Indigenous villages, glaciers, and wildlife in one of the harshest environments on Earth.

CRUISE-TOUR

A cruise tour in Alaska is a combination of a cruise and a land tour that provides a comprehensive experience of the state. It typically begins with a cruise along the Inside Passage or another Alaska cruise route, followed by a land tour that takes passengers to destinations not accessible by ship. During the land portion, passengers will typically stay in hotels and travel by motor coach or train, visiting national parks, glaciers, and other scenic locations.

BRING YOUR CAR CRUISE

For travelers seeking a more choose-your-own-adventure experience in Alaska, the Alaska Marine Highway ferry system is worth looking into. The "Bring Your Car" cruise option allows passengers to bring their own vehicle with them on the ship. The ferry system begins in Bellingham, Washington, and provides access to more than 35 coastal towns in the Inside Passage, Southcentral, and Southwest Alaska.

This option is particularly popular for travelers who want to explore Alaska at their own pace and have more flexibility to go off the beaten path. With this option, passengers can load their car onto the ship at the start of the cruise, and then drive it off the ship at the various ports of call along the way.

JOKES AND SAYINGS ABOUT ALASKAN CRUISES

An Alaskan cruise is a pretty memorable experience, and for those who have been, I'm sure you could agree. Here are a few sayings that may remind you of the more humorous Alaskan cruise moments.

"On an Alaskan cruise, the only thing more majestic than the mountains is the buffet line."

"An Alaskan cruise is like a week-long game of dress-up, where you get to wear all your warmest clothes at once."

"Cruising to Alaska is like taking a vacation from summer and spending a week in the world's biggest refrigerator."

"An Alaskan cruise is a great opportunity to practice your animal impressions—just watch out for the real thing!"

"On an Alaskan cruise, the only thing that moves faster than the glaciers is the line for the hot tub."

"On an Alaskan cruise, you can get closer to nature than you ever wanted to—just ask the guy who got sneezed on by a humpback whale."

"An Alaskan cruise is a great way to bond with your family—

nothing brings people together quite like being trapped on a boat in the middle of nowhere."

"If you're looking for a vacation where the views are breathtaking and the weather is bone-chilling, then an Alaskan cruise is for you!"

"On an Alaskan cruise, you'll have plenty of opportunities to bond with your fellow passengers over shared experiences, like getting lost in Ketchikan or eating way too much at the midnight buffet."

"An Alaskan cruise is like a floating snow globe—except the snowflakes are whales and the glitter is icebergs."

Alaska By Train

Seeing Alaska by train is a great way to see the rugged and spectacular scenic state.

TWO HISTORIC RAILROADS

The Alaska Railroad and the White Pass & Yukon Route Railroad are two historic railroads that offer scenic train rides through the stunning landscape of Alaska and the Yukon. They are a must-see for anyone interested in history, scenic beauty, and adventure.

THE ALASKA RAILROAD

The Alaska Railroad is a state-owned rail system that runs from Seward on the Kenai Peninsula to Fairbanks, passing through scenic areas such as the Chugach and Talkeetna Mountains, as well as glaciers and wildlife preserves. The Alaska Railroad provides daily passenger service during the summer months, and offers a variety of scenic and adventure train tours, including wildlife viewing excursions, glacier trekking, and scenic day trips.

GLASS-DOMED RAIL CARS

Glass-domed rail cars in Alaska. Photo by Drew Farwell on Unsplash.

The Alaska Railroad is famed for its glass-domed rail cars and excellent service. The cars feature large glass dome roofs that allow passengers to enjoy panoramic views of the surrounding landscape as they travel.

The glass-domed rail cars typically have comfortable, plush seating, and are climate-controlled for the comfort of passengers, even during the warm summer months or the chilly fall and winter seasons. They also offer plenty of space for passengers to move around and take in the views from different angles.

THE WHITE PASS & YUKON ROUTE RAILROAD

The White Pass & Yukon Route Railroad is a narrow-gauge railroad that runs from Skagway, Alaska, to Whitehorse, capital of the Canadian Yukon Territory. The railroad was built during the Klondike Gold Rush in the late 1800s and has been in continuous operation ever since.

Today, the White Pass & Yukon Route Railroad is a popular tourist attraction, offering scenic train rides through the rugged and breathtaking landscapes of the Klondike region, including glaciers, snow-capped peaks, and pristine wilderness.

ONBOARD NARRATION

Many of the scenic train rides offered by the White Pass & Yukon Route Railroad feature onboard narrators who provide information about the history and geography of the area, as well as wildlife sightings and other points of interest along the way.

JOKES AND SAYINGS ABOUT TRAVELING ALASKA BY TRAIN

Traveling by train is a unique experience in itself, but traveling by train in Alaska is on a whole other level. Here are a few sayings that express the funny side of Alaska train travel.

"Riding the train in Alaska is like taking a trip through time— you'll feel like you're in the Wild West, except instead of cowboys, there are moose."

"Traveling by train in Alaska is like taking a sightseeing tour of a snow globe."

"On an Alaskan train, the scenery is breathtaking and the train itself is ... well, it's a train."

"Taking the train in Alaska is a great way to see the state's natural beauty up close—just be prepared to get up close and personal with some wildlife too!"

"If you're looking for a way to slow down and appreciate the journey, then traveling by train in Alaska is the perfect option— just don't be surprised if the journey takes a little longer than expected."

"Traveling by train in Alaska is like being on a giant conveyor belt of natural beauty, with occasional stops for hot cocoa and photo ops."

"Traveling by train in Alaska is a great way to experience the state's rugged wilderness without having to rough it too much— unless, of course, you count having to walk to the dining car as 'roughing it.'"

"If you want to see Alaska in all its glory, then riding the train is the way to go—just be prepared for some 'unique' smells and sounds along the way."

Alaska By Car

There are a lot of places in Alaska that you can't see by car because they can only be accessed by plane or boat. But there are a lot of gorgeous drives to take if you decide to road-trip it in Alaska.

. . .

The Alaska Highway: The Alaska Highway is a 1,387-mile highway that connects Alaska to the contiguous United States via Yukon Territory and British Columbia. It passes through some of the North's most stunning landscapes, including the remote and rugged wilderness of the Yukon.

The Seward Highway: The Seward Highway is a 125-mile highway that runs from Anchorage to Seward, along the scenic Turnagain Arm. It offers breathtaking views of glaciers, wildlife, and the Chugach Mountains.

The Denali Highway: The Denali Highway is a 135-mile highway that runs from Cantwell to Paxson, through the heart of the Alaska Range. It offers breathtaking views of the Alaskan wilderness, including glaciers, rivers, and peaks, as well as opportunities for wildlife viewing.

The Richardson Highway: The Richardson Highway is a 364-mile highway that runs from Valdez to Fairbanks, through the heart of Alaska. It passes through several scenic areas, including the Wrangell-St. Elias National Park and Preserve, the Chugach National Forest, and the beautiful Copper River Valley.

The Dalton Highway: The Dalton Highway is a 414-mile highway that runs from Livengood to Deadhorse, through some of the most remote and rugged landscapes in Alaska. It offers stunning views of the Brooks Range and the Arctic tundra, as well as opportunities for wildlife viewing and outdoor recreation.

JOKES AND SAYINGS ABOUT DRIVING IN ALASKA

Due to the rugged, remote and spread-out destinations in Alaska, there are several jokes and sayings about driving in Alaska. Here are a few examples:

"In Alaska, if you're not the lead dog, the view never changes."

———

"In Alaska, the four seasons are: almost winter, winter, still winter, and road construction."

———

"In Alaska, the road less traveled is because it's still under construction."

———

"In Alaska, the shortest distance between two points is not always a straight line."

———

"In Alaska, the potholes are so big, you could lose a car in them."

"In Alaska, the only way to avoid road construction is to drive on the tundra."

"In Alaska, if you drive too slow, you'll get stuck in the mud. If you drive too fast, you'll get stuck in the snow."

"In Alaska, it's not the destination that takes a long time, it's the getting there."

"In Alaska, road trips are measured in hours, not miles."

"In Alaska, it's not about the destination, it's about the journey— and the wildlife sightings along the way."

Alaska By Plane aka Flightseeing

About 75 percent of Alaska's communities can only be reached by air. Planes are used to transport people, goods, and supplies to remote communities that are not accessible by road, as well as for air taxi services, air ambulance services, and medical evacuations.

. . .

Whether by large commercial plane, bush plane or sea plane, getting around by air is an important and common part of Alaska life.

JOKES AND SAYINGS ABOUT TRAVELING BY BUSH PLANE

Here are a few fun jokes and sayings that highlight the unique and adventurous experience of flying by bush plane in Alaska, as well as the often bumpy and wild nature of the flights, which are known for their stunning aerial views of the state's rugged terrain and scenic beauty.

"In Alaska, the only way to avoid road construction is to fly."

"In Alaska, the only thing scarier than flying in a bush plane is landing in a bush plane."

"In Alaska, when you ask for a window seat, you get an unobstructed view of the wilderness ... or the clouds."

"In Alaska, the flight attendant's announcement is, 'Welcome aboard and hold on tight.'"

"In Alaska, the turbulence is just the pilot avoiding the trees."

"In Alaska, the pilot is not only your captain, but also your tour guide."

"In Alaska, the flight is always bumpy, but the view is always breathtaking."

"In Alaska, the only time a pilot says 'This is going to be a smooth flight' is when he's about to land on a river.

24

LEARN TO SPEAK ALASKAN

ALCAN

This is short for the Alaska-Canada Highway. The Alcan is a highway that runs through Alaska and British Columbia, connecting the state of Alaska to the rest of North America. The highway was built during World War II to provide a land route between Alaska and the lower 48 states for military purposes.

BLOWDOWN

An area of trees where several have fallen due to the wind makes a great place to look for trees to use as firewood.

BLUE CANOES

Another word for the blue Alaska Marine Highway ferries.

· · ·

BREAK-UP

In Alaska, the "break-up" happens when frozen rivers and lakes thaw in late spring, marking the end of winter and the start of boating season. Locals and tourists look forward to the break-up as a sign of spring and a chance to see the beauty of the Alaskan wilderness.

The opposite of the break-up is the "freeze-up."

BUNNY BOOTS

Oversized insulated rubber boots that come in white and black. The white ones are traditionally called Bunny Boots, while the sleek black ones are sometimes called Mickey Mouse Boots. They'll keep your feet warm down to -70°F (-56°C).

CHEECHAKO

Cheechako is a term for a newcomer to Alaska, especially one who doesn't have the appropriate skills or understanding of the Alaskan wilderness.

CHINOOK

This term—the name of the Indigenous peoples who tradition-ally lived around the Columbia River in the Pacific Northwest—in Alaska usually refers to a type of salmon, also known as the King salmon, that is highly prized for its rich flavor and oily flesh. It's one of the largest species of salmon.

.   .   .

COMBAT FISHING

Combat fishing is a term used to describe the frantic and often aggressive experience of fishing for salmon in the popular fishing grounds near the Kenai River in Alaska. Fishing is often crowded and highly competitive in these areas, with anglers packed together on the riverbanks and jockeying for the best spots.

DIP NETTING

A popular way to catch fish is simply dipping a net attached to a long pole into the water.

DOWN SOUTH

When Alaskans refer to down south, they're referring to all of the other US states that are all south of Alaska.

FREEZE-UP

In Alaska, freeze-up happens when rivers, lakes, and water-ways freeze over in very cold temperatures. This usually happens in late fall or early winter and lasts until spring or early summer. It signals the start of winter and the end of the boating season.

.   .   .

The opposite of freeze-up is break-up, when the ice melts as temperatures rise.

FROST HEAVES

Frost heaves are a common phenomenon in Alaska and other cold climates. They occur when the ground freezes and thaws, causing the soil to expand and contract. Over time, this repeated expansion and contraction can cause the ground to rise and fall, creating a series of bumps or "heaves" on the surface. Frost heaves are most commonly found on roads, sidewalks, and other paved surfaces and can make travel difficult and uncomfortable.

LAND YACHT

Another name for massive and slow motorhomes or recreational vehicles that can seem to take up the whole road and make it difficult and sometimes unsafe to pass.

LOWER 48

The Lower 48 refers to all of the continental US states—basically all of the other states, other than Hawaii.

MUKLUKS

Pronounced MUCK-lucks, this refers to fur boots. The word comes from maklak, the Yupik word for "bearded."

. . .

MUKTUK

Muktuck, pronounced MUCK-tuck, is the anglicized version of the Inupiaq word maktak, which means whale skin with fat. It's considered a delicacy and is high in protein, fat and vitamins.

MUSKEG

Muskeg is a mixture of bog and swamp covering much of Alaska. It has a spongy texture that makes it difficult to walk or drive on.

NANOOK (naa-NOOK)

The Inupiaq word for polar bear, after which the University of Alaska Fairbanks sports teams are named. It is sometimes used in reference to long-time Alaskans.

OOSIK

An oosik is the bone of the walrus penis. Every year the Alaska Travel Industry Association gives out the Golden Oosik Award to the company that makes the biggest advertising mistake or blunder.

OUTSIDE/GOING OUTSIDE/OUTSIDERS

Outside means anywhere outside of Alaska. Going outside typically refers to leaving the state of Alaska to travel to the contiguous United States or other parts of the world. Similarly, outsiders is often used to refer to people who are not from Alaska, especially those who have recently moved to the state.

SNOWMACHINE

Most of the world knows them as snowmobiles, but they are also referred to as sleds. Snowmachines are a common way to get around during the winter in Alaska.

SOURDOUGH

The opposite of a cheechako is a sourdough. This person has lived in Alaska for a long time. During the gold rush days, sourdoughs were individuals known for their self-sufficient nature and their ability to survive and thrive in the harsh Alaskan wilderness.

TERMINATION DUST

In Alaska, the first snowfall of the year is called termination dust, which signifies the end of the season and the arrival of winter. It refers to the dusting of snow that settles on the mountaintops, marking the termination of summer.

ULU (Oo-loo)

An ulu is a traditional Alaska Native cutting tool, similar to a knife. It typically has a semi-circular curved blade with a handle on one end. It is used for various tasks such as skinning animals, chopping vegetables, and filleting fish.

· · ·

UP NORTH

For those living in Southeast Alaska, "Up North" means main-land Alaska.

VISQUEEN

Waterproof plastic sheeting that's cheap and effective at blocking wind and rain and is used to wrap pretty much anything and everything. To protect vegetable seedlings in the spring, Visqueen is also often used to construct temporary greenhouses.

25

ODD ALASKAN LAWS

Reading about some old laws is like reading the warning labels on common products and realizing that someone was stupid enough to do whatever it was they're warning you not to do. In this case, these transgressions were serious enough to make them into serious offenses and laws. Every state has their own set of odd laws.

Here are a few of Alaska's:

NO PUSHING MOOSE OUT OF AIRPLANES

In Alaska, it is illegal to push a live moose out of a moving airplane. This law is in place to protect both the moose and the people on the ground. The law was enacted in 1994 after several instances of moose being pushed out of planes as a form of wildlife management.

. . .

ILLEGAL TO VIEW MOOSE FROM AN AIRPLANE

That is to say, you can't view moose from an airplane and then hunt them the same day. Alaska has some strong regulations in place to prevent hunters from using airplanes to locate and kill game animals, which is seen as unsportsmanlike and unethical.

WAKING A SLEEPING BEAR FOR A PHOTO

It is against the law in Alaska to wake a sleeping bear for the purpose of taking a photograph.

(Alaska Statute Title 16 Fish and Game; Chapter 05). Even if it wasn't illegal, it should be, because it's dangerous and irresponsible.

NO ROAMING THE CITY WITH YOUR BOW AND ARROWS

Having and discharging a bow and arrow or slingshot, among other devices that shoot out objects, is not allowed within city limits in Alaska.

YOU MUST HAVE A PERMIT FOR YOUR CONCEALED SLINGSHOT

While it's fairly normal to have a permit for other concealed weapons, it is a bit unusual to include a slingshot as one of those weapons.

. . .

MAKE SURE THE HOUSE TRAILER IS EMPTY BEFORE MOVING

It's a ticketable offense to move a house trailer on public roads with a person inside.

NO BUILDING A SNOWMAN TALLER THAN YOU ON SCHOOL PROPERTY

Children are not allowed to build snowmen that are taller than themselves when they are on school property. Due to large amount of snow Alaska can get, this law was put into place so rescue workers and school administrators could differentiate between snowmen and actual children.

26

QUOTABLES & QUIRKY ALASKA-ISMS

Quotes

"To the lover of wilderness, Alaska is one of the most wonderful countries in the world."
— John Muir, *Travels in Alaska*

"The most glorious of all the terrestrial manifestations of God."
– John Muir, describing Alaska's Northern Lights

"For sheer majestic geography and sublime scale, nothing beats Alaska and the Yukon." – Sam Abell, National Geographic photographer

---

"Alaska has long been a magnet for dreamers and misfits, people who think the unsullied enormity of the Last Frontier will patch all the holes in their lives. The bush is an unforgiving place, however, that cares nothing for hope or longing. – Jon Krakauer, author

---

"Moose are the squirrels of Alaska." – Tim Moon

Alaska Sayings & Quirky Alaska-isms

"Alaska is a state of mind, a place where dreams are born and memories are made." – Unknown

---

"Alaska is a place of adventure, where the wild and the unknown still exist." – Unknown

---

"In Alaska, the nights are long, the days are short, and the memories are forever." – Unknown

---

"Alaska is where the spirit of the wild still roams free." – Unknown

---

"The beauty of Alaska is not just in its landscape, but in the hearts of its people." – Unknown

---

"In Alaska, if it's not snowing, it's raining. And if it's not raining, it's snowing." – Unknown

---

"Alaska is where Mother Nature let her hair down and went a little wild." – Unknown

---

"In Alaska, we measure distance in hours, not miles." – Unknown

---

"Alaska: Where the men are men and the women win the Iditarod."

"In Alaska, we have two seasons: winter and construction."

"Alaskans: because we like to live life on the edge (of the continent)."

———

"In Alaska, we don't tan, we rust."

———

"Alaska: where the animals outnumber the people and the winters outnumber the summers."

———

"You know you're in Alaska when the snowplows have names like Grizzly and Polar Bear."

———

"Alaska: where the winters are long, the summers are short, and the mosquitoes are huge."

———

"You know you're in Alaska when the local coffee shop has a drive-thru for snowmobiles."

———

27

QUIZ YOURSELF

1. What is Termination Dust?

A. The snow that's kicked up by a dogsled team when they run past
B. What Alaskans call the first snowfall of the year
C. Another word for moose droppings
D. Thick and heavy Alaskan fog

2. What is the capital of Alaska?

A. Fairbanks
B. Sitka
C. Juneau
D. Anchorage

3. What is the tallest mountain in Alaska?

A. Mount Logan
B. Denali

C. Mount Saint Elias

D. Mount Foraker

4. Alaska has two official state holidays; what are they?

A. Alaska Day and Seward's Day

B. Summer and Winter Solstice

C. The Day the River Opens and Dividend Day

D. Alaska Day and Dividend Day

5. Which dessert is unique to Alaska?

A. Baked Alaska

B. Akutaq

C. Neapolitan ice cream

D. Beaver Tails

6. Which of these towns is where the famous Iditarod Dog Sled Race finishes?

A. Anchorage

B. Nome

C. Fairbanks

D. Ketchikan

7. Alaskan polar bears and grizzly bears have been known to mate, and their hybrid offspring are called grolar bears and pizzly bears.

A. True

B. False

8. The Alaskan Flag was designed by a 14-year-old boy as part of a contest.

A. True
B. False

9. Alaska is the 50th US state.

A. True
B. False

10. There are 21 official languages in Alaska.

A. True
B. False

11. There are more women than men in Alaska.

A. True
B. False

12. What is Fat Bear Week in Alaska?

A. A week-long celebration of the hunting season and the state's outdoor lifestyle
B. The week between Christmas and New Year's Day, when it's common to eat a lot
C. A social media contest that invites people to vote on which bears in Katmai National Park are the fattest
D. An annual gathering of scientists and researchers to study the effects of climate change on polar bears

13. What is Alaska's official state sport?

A. Fishing
B. Dog mushing
C. Hunting
D. Snowmachine racing

14. What is Alaska's state land mammal?

A. Grizzly bear
B. Moose
C. Gray wolf
D. Reindeer

15. Which of these famous singers is from Alaska?

A. Tom Jones
B. Jewel
C. Taylor Swift
D. John Denver

16. Alaska is in two hemispheres.

A. True
B. False

17. Alaska has never had temperatures exceeding 100°F, or 37.8°C.

A. True
B. False

18. Polar bears are considered a marine mammal.

A. True
B. False

19. In Alaska, hikers have to be especially careful of poison oak and poison ivy.

A. True
B. False

20. How many time zones does Alaska have?

A. One
B. Two
C. Three
D. Four

28

QUIZ ANSWERS

1. What is Termination Dust?

A. The snow that's kicked up by a dogsled team when they run past

B. What Alaskans call the first snowfall of the year

C. Another word for moose droppings

D. Thick and heavy Alaskan fog

2. What is the capital of Alaska?

A. Fairbanks

B. Sitka

C. Juneau

D. Anchorage

3. What is the tallest mountain in Alaska?

A. Mount Logan
B. Denali
C. Mount Saint Elias
D. Mount Foraker

4. Alaska has two official state holidays; what are they?

A. Alaska Day and Seward's Day
B. Summer and Winter Solstice
C. The Day the River Opens and Dividend Day
D. Alaska Day and Dividend Day

5. Which dessert is unique to Alaska?

A. Baked Alaska
B. Akutaq
C. Neapolitan ice cream
D. Beaver Tails

6. Which of these towns is where the famous Iditarod Dog Sled Race finishes?

A. Anchorage
B. Nome
C. Fairbanks
D. Ketchikan

7. Alaskan polar bears and grizzly bears have been known to mate, and their hybrid offspring are called grolar bears and pizzly bears.

A. True

B. False

8. The Alaskan Flag was designed by a 14-year-old boy as part of a contest.

A. True

B. False

9. Alaska is the 50th US state.

A. True

B. False

10. There are 21 official languages in Alaska.

A. True

B. False

11. There are more women than men in Alaska.

A. True

B. False

12. What is Fat Bear Week in Alaska?

A. A week-long celebration of the hunting season and the state's outdoor lifestyle

B. The week between Christmas and New Year's Day, when it's common to eat a lot

C. A social media contest that invites people

to vote on which bears in Katmai National Park are the fattest
D. An annual gathering of scientists and researchers to study the effects of climate change on polar bears

13. What is Alaska's official state sport?

A. Fishing
B. Dog mushing
C. Hunting
D. Snowmachine racing

14. What is Alaska's state land mammal?

A. Grizzly bear
B. Moose
C. Gray wolf
D. Reindeer

15. Which of these famous singers is from Alaska?

A. Tom Jones
B. Jewel
C. Taylor Swift
D. John Denver

16. Alaska is in two hemispheres.

A. True
B. False

17. Alaska has never had temperatures exceeding 100°F, or 37.8°C.

   A. True
   B. False

18. Polar bears are considered a marine mammal.

   A. True
   B. False

19. In Alaska, hikers have to be especially careful of poison oak and poison ivy.

   A. True
   B. False

20. How many time zones does Alaska have?

   A. One
   B. Two
   C. Three
   D. Four

LEARN SOMETHING? PLEASE LEAVE A REVIEW

If you enjoyed this book, please share your thoughts in a REVIEW. Your sincere feedback is really helpful and I would love to hear from you!

Please leave a quick review on
Amazon at
bit.ly/alaska-book-review

If Goodreads is more your thing, please share it there.
www.goodreads.com

Thank you so very much!

DON'T FORGET YOUR FREE SPECIAL BONUS

As a special bonus and as a **thank you for purchasing this book**, I created a FREE companion quiz e-book with over 100 fun questions and answers taken from this book.

Test your knowledge of Alaska and quiz your friends.

It's all FREE.

Download your bonus quiz e-book here:

http://bit.ly/alaskabook-bonus

Enjoy!

ABOUT THE AUTHOR

Marianne Jennings is a self-proclaimed adventure craver and an adventure addict. She proudly holds the title of favorite aunt to her ten nieces and nephews, and is a lover of new foods and new experiences.

She loves facts and trivia like Alaskans love their XTRATUF boots and cloudberries. To help introduce other places, people, and cultures to others, she likes to share interesting and fun facts that are entertaining and memorable.

If you'd like to learn more or join her mailing list, you can connect with Marianne at https://knowledgenuggetbooks.com or on Instagram.

instagram.com/knowledgenuggetbooks

ALSO BY MARIANNE JENNINGS

So You Think You Know Canada, Eh?

Gold Medal Winner and **#1 Bestseller** in both Canadian Travel & Trivia and Fun Facts – This collection of silly & interesting facts is about Canada, the kind people who live there, all things maple syrup, hockey & lacrosse, its unique history, the breathtaking nature, & words to help you speak Canadian.

Available as a paperback and ebook.

Everything About Astronauts Vol. 1 & Vol. 2

Teens and adults who love astronauts, fun facts, and little-known stories will find themselves mesmerized with over 1,400 interesting facts and out-of-world stories.

Available as a paperback and ebook.

Made in the USA
Columbia, SC
13 June 2024